A BALANCED MATHEMATICS PROGRAM INTEGRATING SCIENCE AND LANGUAGE ARTS

Unit Resource Guide
Unit 4

Division and Data

THIRD EDITION

KENDALL/HUNT PUBLISHING COMPANY
4050 Westmark Drive   Dubuque, Iowa 52002

A TIMS® Curriculum
University of Illinois at Chicago

UIC The University of Illinois at Chicago

The original edition was based on work supported by the National Science Foundation under grant No. MDR 9050226 and the University of Illinois at Chicago. Any opinions, findings, and conclusions or recommendations expressed in this publication are those of the author(s) and do not necessarily reflect the views of the granting agencies.

Letter Home

Division and Data

Date: _____

Dear Family Member:

In this unit, your child will find the areas of shapes and divide using one-digit divisors. Using these skills, he or she will average data and practice estimation. Students also participate in a lab experience, *Spreading Out*.

The paper-and-pencil method that *Math Trailblazers*® uses to do long division is somewhat different from the way long division is traditionally taught in the United States. This method, called the forgiving division method, is often easier for students to learn. They do not have to erase as much, and they learn more about division and estimation.

```
        92
  7 | 644
    - 140      20
      504
      350      50
      154
      140      20
       14
       14       2
        0       92
```

The forgiving division method is often easier for children to learn.

As we work together in class, these are some ways to help your child at home:

- Encourage your child to show you how he or she is learning division.
- Talk about measuring area in your home. For example, you might discuss the number of square feet in different rooms in your home.
- Ask your child to tell you more about the lab *Spreading Out*.
- Help your child study the multiplication and division facts at home. In this unit, we work with the square numbers (2×2, 3×3, 4×4, etc.). Use the *Triangle Flash Cards* to help review the facts.

Thank you for your support.

Sincerely,

_____

Carta al hogar

División y datos

Fecha: _____

Estimado miembro de familia:

En esta unidad, su hijo/a hallará las áreas de figuras y dividirá usando divisores de un dígito. Usando estas habilidades, su hijo/a hallará promedios de datos y practicará la estimación. Los estudiantes también participarán en una experiencia de laboratorio titulada Expandiendo.

El método de papel y lápiz que usa *Math Trailblazers*® para hacer la división larga es un poco diferente al modo tradicional que se enseña en los Estados Unidos. Este método, llamado método de división "que perdona", suele ser más fácil de aprender para los estudiantes. No tienen que borrar tanto, y aprenden más sobre división y estimación. Mientras trabajamos juntos en clase, éstas son algunas maneras en las que usted puede ayudar a su hijo/a en casa:

```
            92
    7 |  644
      -  140      20
         504
         350      50
         154
         140      20
          14
          14       2
           0      92
```

El método de división "que perdona" suele ser más fácil de aprendar para los niños.

- Animando a su hijo/a a que le enseñe cómo está aprendiendo a dividir.

- Hablando acerca de medir áreas en su casa. Por ejemplo, pueden hablar sobre el número de pies cuadrados en diferentes habitaciones de la casa.

- Pidiéndole a su hijo/a que le cuente más acerca de la experiencia de laboratorio Expandiendo.

- Ayudando a su hijo a estudiar las tablas de multiplicación y división en casa. En esta unidad, trabajamos con los números al cuadrado (2×2, 3×3, 4×4, etc.). Use las tarjetas triangulares para repasar las tablas.

Gracias por su apoyo.

Atentamente,

_____

Table of Contents

Unit 4
Division and Data

Unit 4

Outline
Division and Data

Unit Summary

Estimated Class Sessions
14-20

This unit extends and applies students' knowledge of several topics: division, measuring area, averages (means and medians), and accuracy in measurement and estimation. Division is explored first by modeling with the base-ten pieces, then by using a paper-and-pencil method. Students explore area and use it as a basis for making estimates. In an optional activity, they check the accuracy of their estimates using 10% as a benchmark.

For the first time in fifth grade, students use the mean to average a set of data. The lab *Spreading Out* draws upon many of the concepts in the unit including area and averages. As part of the lab, students decide when it is appropriate to use a bar graph and when it is appropriate to use a point graph. The Adventure Book *George Washington Carver: Man of Measure* explores many of the variables in math and science. A midterm test assesses many of the concepts and skills studied thus far. The DPP for this unit reviews the multiplication and division facts for the square numbers.

Major Concept Focus

- area
- modeling division with base-ten pieces
- choosing appropriate graph
- manipulated, responding, and fixed variables
- interpreting remainders
- estimation
- 10% as a standard for estimation
- averages: medians and means
- *Adventure Book:* variables in math and science
- multiplication and division facts: square numbers
- TIMS Laboratory Method
- paper-and-pencil division
- ratios
- estimating quotients
- point graphs
- best-fit lines
- using ratios
- midterm test
- order of operations

Pacing Suggestions

Students' knowledge of division and familiarity with base-ten pieces will determine how quickly the class can proceed through Lessons 2 and 3, which review division concepts and a paper-and-pencil method for division. Students will have numerous opportunities to practice paper-and-pencil division during activities, laboratory investigations, Daily Practice and Problems, and Home Practice assignments in this and subsequent units.

The unit includes two optional lessons:

- Lesson 4 *How Close Is Close Enough?* discusses accuracy in measurement. Students learn to use 10% as a benchmark to judge the accuracy of their measurements. This concept is then applied in the *Spreading Out* laboratory investigation in this unit, as well as in laboratory investigations and Daily Practice and Problems items in future units. If you elect to skip this activity, you will need to skip related questions in subsequent lessons. In *Spreading Out,* skip **Questions 10C** and **11C.**

- The second optional lesson, Lesson 8 *Review Problems,* prepares students for the *Midterm Test,* the last activity in this unit. You can distribute *Review Problems* as homework throughout the unit rather than as an in-class review.

- To move through the unit more quickly, use *Math Trailblazers* connections to other subjects. For example, use science time to collect data for the *Spreading Out* lab. The *Adventure Book* on George Washington Carver can be linked with language arts or social studies instruction.

Assessment Indicators

Use the following Assessment Indicators and the *Observational Assessment Record* that follows the Background section in this unit to assess students on key ideas.

A1. Can students measure area?

A2. Can students find the median and mean of a data set?

A3. Can students divide with 1-digit divisors using paper and pencil?

A4. Can students estimate quotients?

A5. Can students interpret remainders?

A6. Can students divide numbers with ending zeros mentally?

A7. Can students draw and interpret best-fit lines?

A8. Can students collect, organize, graph, and analyze data?

A9. Do students demonstrate fluency with the multiplication and division facts for the square numbers?

Unit Planner

KEY: SG = Student Guide, DAB = Discovery Assignment Book, AB = Adventure Book, URG = Unit Resource Guide, DPP = Daily Practice and Problems, HP = Home Practice (found in Discovery Assignment Book), and TIG = Teacher Implementation Guide.

	Lesson Information	Supplies	Copies/Transparencies

Lesson 1
Grid Area

URG Pages 32–51
SG Pages 102–105
DAB Pages 49–63

DPP A–D
HP Parts 1–2

Estimated Class Sessions
2

Activity
Students find areas of figures drawn on *Centimeter Grid Paper.* They discover strategies for finding the area of shapes with straight sides and for estimating the area of shapes with curved sides.

Math Facts
Complete DPP item B and begin reviewing the multiplication and division facts for the square numbers.

Homework
1. Assign the *Finding Area* and *Cut and Paste Puzzles* Homework Pages in the *Discovery Assignment Book.*
2. Assign the Homework section in the *Student Guide.*
3. Assign Parts 1 and 2 of the Home Practice.

Assessment
1. Use the *Observational Assessment Record* to record students' abilities to find the area of a shape.
2. Use the *Finding Area* Activity Page as an assessment.
3. Use DPP item D as a short assessment.

Supplies:
• 1 ruler per student
• 1 pair of scissors per student
• glue

Copies/Transparencies:
• 3–4 copies of *Centimeter Grid Paper* URG Page 44 per student
• 1 transparency of *Centimeter Grid Paper* URG Page 44
• 1 transparency of *Under the Rug* DAB Page 53
• 1 copy of *Observational Assessment Record* URG Pages 13–14 to be used throughout this unit

Lesson 2
Modeling Division

URG Pages 52–67
SG Pages 106–112

DPP E–H

Estimated Class Sessions
2

Activity
Students model division problems with base-ten pieces. Estimation is stressed.

Math Facts
Complete item E and continue reviewing the multiplication and division facts for the square numbers.

Homework
Assign Homework *Questions 1–15* in the *Student Guide.*

Assessment
Use the *Observational Assessment Record* to record students' abilities to model division with base-ten pieces.

Supplies:
• 1 calculator per student
• 1 set of base-ten pieces (2 packs, 14 flats, 30 skinnies, 50 bits) per student pair
• overhead base-ten pieces, optional

Copies/Transparencies:
• 1 table from *Multiplication Table* URG Page 61 per student
• copies of *Base-Ten Pieces Masters* URG Pages 62–63 as needed

Lesson 3
Paper-and-Pencil Division

URG Pages 68–79
SG Pages 113–117

DPP I–N
HP Part 3

Estimated Class Sessions
3

Activity
Students solve division problems using a paper-and-pencil method called the forgiving method.

Math Facts
Complete DPP items I, K, and M and continue reviewing the multiplication and division facts for the square numbers.

Homework
1. Assign the Homework section in the *Student Guide* over several nights.
2. Assign Part 3 of the Home Practice.

Assessment
Students complete the *Quiz* Assessment Page.

Supplies:
• 1 calculator per student
• 1 set of base-ten pieces (2 packs, 14 flats, 30 skinnies, 50 bits) per student pair
• overhead base-ten pieces, optional

Copies/Transparencies:
• 1 copy of *Quiz* URG Page 76 per student

	Lesson Information	Supplies	Copies/ Transparencies
Lesson 4 **How Close Is Close Enough?** URG Pages 80–96 SG Pages 118–122 DAB Page 65 *Estimated Class Sessions* **2-3**	OPTIONAL LESSON **Optional Activity** Students learn to find 10% of a number and use 10% as a standard for error analysis. **Homework** Assign the Homework section in the *Student Guide*.	• 1 calculator per student	• 1 copy of *Shapes 1–5* URG Page 91 per student • 1 copy of *Shapes 6 and 7* URG Page 92 per student • 1 copy of *Two-column Data Table* URG Page 93 per student group • 1 transparency of *Shapes 1–5* URG Page 91 • 1 transparency of *10% Chart* DAB Page 65 or large graph paper for a class data table • 1 transparency of *Centimeter Grid Paper* URG Page 44, optional • 1 transparency of *Two-column Data Table* URG Page 93, optional
Lesson 5 **Mean or Median?** URG Pages 97–109 SG Pages 123–130 DPP O–R *Estimated Class Sessions* **2**	**Activity** Students review methods for finding the mean value for a set of data. They compare mean and median. **Math Facts** Continue reviewing the multiplication and division facts for the square numbers. **Homework** Assign the Homework section in the *Student Guide*. **Assessment** Use DPP items Y and Z as quizzes.	• 1 calculator per student • 80 connecting cubes or square-inch tiles per student pair	
Lesson 6 **Spreading Out** URG Pages 110–133 SG Pages 131–138 DPP S–X HP Part 4 *Estimated Class Sessions* **3-4**	**Lab** Students look for the relationship between the number of drops on a paper towel and the area of the spot they create. They use the data to solve problems involving ratios. **Math Facts** Assign DPP item S. Review multiplication and division facts for square numbers. **Homework** 1. Assign the Homework section in the *Student Guide* after Part 3 of the lab. 2. Assign Part 4 of the Home Practice. **Assessment** 1. Use the *Observational Assessment Record* to document students' abilities to measure area and work with data. 2. Use the TIMS *Multidimensional Rubric* to score specific questions from the lab. 3. Use DPP item V as a quiz.	• 1 calculator per student • 1–2 pairs of scissors per student group • 1 eyedropper per student group • 3–4 sheets of the same brand of paper towel per student group • 1 ruler per student • 1 small container of water per student group • 2 books or 1 geoboard (for drying the paper towels) per student group	• 1 copy of *Centimeter Grid Paper* URG Page 44 per student or more as needed • 1 copy of *Three-trial Data Table* URG Page 129 per student or more as needed • 2 copies of *Centimeter Graph Paper* URG Page 130 per student • 1 transparency of *Centimeter Graph Paper* URG Page 130, optional • 1 transparency of *Bar Graph or Point Graph?* URG Page 127, optional • 1 transparency of *Spot Check* URG Page 128, optional

(Continued)

	Lesson Information	Supplies	Copies/Transparencies
	4. Transfer appropriate documentation from the Unit 4 *Observational Assessment Record* to students' *Individual Assessment Record Sheets*.		• 1 copy of *Individual Assessment Record Sheet* TIG Assessment section per student, previously copied for use throughout the year

Lesson 7

George Washington Carver: Man of Measure

URG Pages 134–143
DAB Page 67
AB Pages 21–34

DPP Y–Z

Estimated Class Sessions

1

Adventure Book
Students are introduced to George Washington Carver as he sets up his lab at Tuskegee Institute. He and his students improvise lab equipment to measure length, area, volume, time, and mass.

Math Facts
Assign DPP item Z that reviews math facts using the order of operations.

Homework
Assign the *Variables* Activity Page.

Assessment
1. Have students draw up a plan for making a two-pan balance and use household items to build it.
2. Have students make their own standard masses.
3. Have students test the soil at school or home.

Lesson 8

Review Problems

URG Pages 144–151
SG Pages 139–142

HP Part 5

Estimated Class Sessions

1

OPTIONAL LESSON

Optional Activity
Students solve problems that review concepts on the midterm test.

Math Facts
Continue reviewing the multiplication and division facts for the square numbers.

Homework
1. Assign all or part of this lesson as homework.
2. Assign Part 5 of the Home Practice.

• 1 calculator per student
• pattern blocks
• 1 ruler per student

• 2 copies of *Centimeter Graph Paper* URG Page 130 per student

Lesson 9

Midterm Test

URG Pages 152–164
DPP AA–BB

Estimated Class Sessions

1-2

Assessment Activity
Students take a short-item test that assesses skills and concepts studied in the first four units.

Math Facts
Assign DPP item AA.

• 1 calculator per student
• pattern blocks
• 1 ruler per student

• 2 copies of *Centimeter Graph Paper* URG Page 130 per student
• 1 copy of *Midterm Test* URG Pages 156–161 per student

Students use eyedroppers in Lesson 6. Provide an informal opportunity for students to practice using eyedroppers.

Connections

A current list of literature and software connections is available at *www.mathtrailblazers.com*. You can also find information on connections in the *Teacher Implementation Guide* Literature List and Software List sections.

Literature Connections

Suggested Titles

- Adair, Gene. *George Washington Carver: Botanist.* Chelsea House Publishers, New York, 1989. (Lesson 7)
- Carter, Andy, and Carol Saller. *George Washington Carver.* Carolrhoda Books, Inc., Minneapolis, MN, 2001. (Lesson 7)
- Dodds, Dayle Ann. *The Great Divide: A Mathematical Marathon.* Candlewick Press, Cambridge, MA, 1999.
- Mitchel, Barbara. *A Pocketful of Goobers.* Carolrhoda Books, Inc., Minneapolis, MN, 1989. (Lesson 7)
- Moore, Eva. *The Story of George Washington Carver.* Scholastic, New York, 1995. (Lesson 7)

Software Connections

- *The Factory Deluxe* promotes spatial reasoning and practices finding area.
- *Graph Master* allows students to collect data and create their own graphs. (Lesson 6)
- *Ice Cream Truck* develops problem solving, money skills, and arithmetic operations.
- *Math Mysteries: Advanced Whole Numbers* is a series of structured multistep word problems dealing with whole numbers.
- *Mighty Math Calculating Crew* poses short answer questions about number operations.
- *Mighty Math Number Heroes* poses short answer questions about number operations.
- *National Library of Virtual Manipulatives* website (http://matti.usu.edu) allows students to work with manipulatives including geoboards, base-ten pieces, the abacus, and many others.
- *Number Sense and Problem Solving: How the West Was One + Three × Four* provides practice in the order of operations.
- *TinkerPlots* allows students to record, compare, and analyze data in tables and graphs.

Teaching All Math Trailblazers Students

Math Trailblazers lessons are designed for students with a wide range of abilities. The lessons are flexible and do not require significant adaptation for diverse learning styles or academic levels. However, when needed, lessons can be tailored to allow students to engage their abilities to the greatest extent possible while building knowledge and skills.

To assist you in meeting the needs of all students in your classroom, this section contains information about some of the features in the curriculum that allow all students access to mathematics. For additional information, see the Teaching the *Math Trailblazers* Student: Meeting Individual Needs section in the *Teacher Implementation Guide.*

Differentiation Opportunities in this Unit

Laboratory Experiments

Laboratory experiments enable students to solve problems using a variety of representations including pictures, tables, graphs, and symbols. Teachers can assign or adapt parts of the analysis according to the student's ability. The following lesson is a lab:

- Lesson 6 *Spreading Out*

Journal Prompts

Journal prompts provide opportunities for students to explain and reflect on mathematical problems. They can help both students who need practice explaining their ideas and students who benefit from answering higher order questions. Students with various learning styles can express themselves using pictures, words, and sentences. Teachers can alter journal prompts to suit students' ability levels. The following lessons contain a journal prompt:

- Lesson 1 *Grid Area*
- Lesson 4 *How Close Is Close Enough?*

DPP Challenges

DPP Challenges are items from the Daily Practice and Problems that usually take more than fifteen minutes to complete. These problems are more thought-provoking and can be used to stretch students' problem-solving skills. The following lessons have DPP Challenges in them:

- DPP Challenge L from Lesson 3 *Paper-and-Pencil Division*
- DPP Challenge P from Lesson 5 *Mean or Median?*
- DPP Challenges T and X from Lesson 6 *Spreading Out*
- DPP Challenge BB from Lesson 9 *Midterm Test*

Extensions

Use extensions to enrich lessons. Many extensions provide opportunities to further involve or challenge students of all abilities. Take a moment to review the extensions prior to beginning this unit. Some extensions may require additional preparation and planning. The following lessons contain extensions:

- Lesson 1 *Grid Area*
- Lesson 3 *Paper-and-Pencil Division*
- Lesson 5 *Mean or Median?*
- Lesson 6 *Spreading Out*
- Lesson 7 *George Washington Carver: Man of Measure*
- Lesson 9 *Midterm Test*

Background
Division and Data

This unit extends and applies students' knowledge of several topics: division, area, averages (means and medians), and accuracy in measurement and estimation.

Division

In Grade 4, students modeled division problems using base-ten pieces and began work with paper-and-pencil methods. In this unit, students use base-ten pieces to build a conceptual model of division as equal sharing. This type of division is referred to as **measurement division.** The number of groups and the total number of objects in the set are known. An example: Ms. Jones drove 144 miles in 6 trips of equal distance. How many miles did she drive each trip? Practice problems also include the other type of division situation known as equal grouping or **partitive division.** In this type of division, the number in each group and the total number are known. Division is used to find the number of groups. For example, a store sells tulip bulbs. The bulbs come in packages of 8. If they sold 216 bulbs, how many packages did they sell?

In this unit, an alternative division method is presented, rather than the one traditionally used in the United States. This method, which we call the **forgiving division method,** does not require that the greatest quotient be found at each step, eliminating the frequent erasing encountered with the standard algorithm. Research shows that students taught the forgiving division method are better at solving unfamiliar problems and better able to explain the meaning of the steps in the method than those taught the traditional method (van Engen and Gibb, 1956). The forgiving division method also gives students the opportunity to practice mental math.

As an example of the forgiving method, we divide 23 into 5256. (Note that even though the example here involves a two-digit divisor, in this unit the division problems involve one-digit divisors. In Unit 9 students will work with two-digit divisors.) There are 5256 marbles to be shared equally among 23 children. How many marbles will each child get? To begin, take a guess, say, 100. Then write:

$$
\begin{array}{r}
23\overline{\smash)5256} \\
-\,2300 \\
\hline
2956
\end{array} \Big| 100
$$

Figure 1: *One possible first step in dividing 23 into 5256*

Students should be encouraged to multiply 23×100 mentally, as discussed in Unit 2. The 2300 is the number of marbles that have been taken care of, with 2956 marbles left to distribute. After subtracting, we see that 100 is a good choice for the next number as well.

$$
\begin{array}{r}
23\overline{\smash)5256} \\
-\,2300 \\
\hline
2956 \\
2300 \\
\hline
656
\end{array} \begin{array}{l} 100 \\ \\ 100 \end{array}
$$

Figure 2: *A second possible step in dividing 23 into 5256*

Students should look at the size of the remainder. They should see that 100 is now too big. That is, we cannot give 100 more marbles to each child. A student might choose 10 here and then 10 again as shown below.

$$
\begin{array}{r}
23\overline{\smash)5256} \\
-\,2300 \\
\hline
2956 \\
2300 \\
\hline
656 \\
230 \\
\hline
426 \\
230 \\
\hline
196
\end{array} \begin{array}{l} 100 \\ \\ 100 \\ \\ 10 \\ \\ 10 \end{array}
$$

Figure 3: *Two more steps in dividing 23 into 5256*

At this point, 5 might be a good choice. See Figure 4.

With 81 remaining, a student might guess too high and choose 4. Only when the guess is too high do you have to erase. The last partial quotient is 3, leaving a remainder of 12. Adding up the number of 23s that divide 5256, we find 228. That is, 23 divides 5256 a total of 228 times with remainder 12. We distributed 228 marbles to each child with 12 left over. The 228 R12 can be written above the divisor as usual. Over time students become better at mental estimation and the number of steps required decreases. The forgiving method closely resembles the traditional method if the best estimate is made at each step.

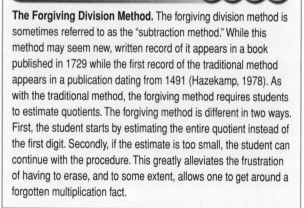

Figure 4: *A final possible step in dividing 23 into 5256*

While this unit and the Daily Practice and Problems provide practice with multiplication and division, a concerted effort is made not to make practice the focal point of work with procedures. Researchers find that spending more time in understanding procedures rather than practicing them aids recall and proficiency in the long run (Hiebert, 1990). Students should practice small numbers of problems for short periods of time spread out throughout the year. While we have chosen one method to teach division, encourage students to share other correct methods of dividing—either those they learned previously, those learned from their parents, or those they invented themselves. Class discussions about other methods can greatly enhance understanding of division and also make clear that problems in mathematics can be solved in many ways.

Area

The **area** of a shape can be defined as the amount of space it covers. Understanding area is important in understanding many real-world situations—whether it is the amount of carpet needed to cover a floor or the structure of our lungs. Area is generally measured in square units. In *Math Trailblazers,* the unit of area measure we use most frequently is the square centimeter. A **square centimeter** (sq cm) is the amount of surface within a square that is 1 cm on each side. See Figure 5.

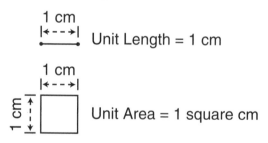

Figure 5: *A square centimeter*

In students' previous work with *Math Trailblazers,* they found the area of various shapes by counting the number of square units that the shape covered. In early grades, students actually cover shapes with square-inch tiles or other, nonstandard units. Often, these shapes are neatly drawn on grids; students first count the number of full square units

and then add the fractional pieces, which generally were either $\frac{1}{2}$ or $\frac{1}{4}$ square units. Beginning in third grade, students find the area of shapes that do not neatly fall onto grid lines. As illustrated in Strategy A in Figure 6, students count whole square units and then put together the remaining pieces, trying to form full square units. The result is a good estimate of the area. Students use this technique in several activities in this unit, including the lab *Spreading Out*. We also encourage students to develop alternative strategies for finding the area of irregular shapes. For example, Strategy B in Figure 6 illustrates a more sophisticated process for finding the area of the shape.

Until now, we have avoided the use of formulas to find area, instead focusing on developing students' conceptual understanding of area. In this unit, we formally introduce the formula for finding the area of a rectangle. We also lay the conceptual groundwork for the introduction in Unit 15 of the formula for finding the area of a triangle. For further discussion of area, refer to the TIMS Tutor: *Area* in the *Teacher Implementation Guide.*

More on Averages

Averages are used throughout *Math Trailblazers* to find a representative value of a data set. Beginning in first grade, students find the median (the "middle" value) of data collected in laboratory experiments and other activities. In fourth grade, students begin using the mean to represent a data set.

Earlier this year, students examined a third kind of average, the mode (the most common value). In this unit, students extend their understanding of averages by analyzing how different kinds of averages sometimes result in varied interpretations of data. For further information about averages, refer to the TIMS Tutor: *Averages* in the *Teacher Implementation Guide.*

How Close Is Close?

Virtually all math educators agree that estimation should be an important part of the math curriculum. As students practice estimation, the question inevitably arises whether the estimate is close to the desired result. This is particularly apparent in the laboratory experiments in *Math Trailblazers* where students often make predictions based on patterns in data and then check their predictions experimentally.

The most fundamental idea about "closeness" is that it is *relative.* For example, suppose two merchants are selling the same item and the prices differ by $1. Whether the prices are close depends upon whether you are buying, for example, a new car for $20,000 or a cup of coffee for $2. As this example points out, when comparing the closeness of numbers or measurements, we need to look at the ratio of the two numbers rather than the difference. This, however, is difficult for fifth-grade students to understand fully, requiring time and exposure to many experiences. We deal with this problem in *Math Trailblazers* in two ways.

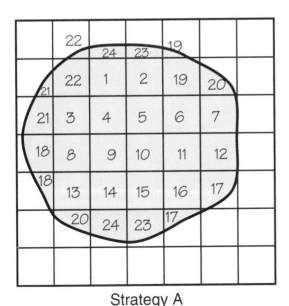
Strategy A

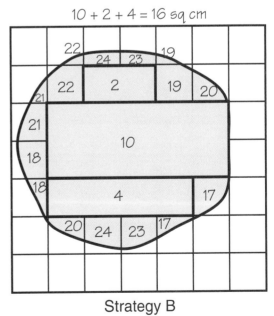
Strategy B

Figure 6: *Strategies for finding the area of irregular shapes*

1. Instead of using ratios, we use a related concept—percent.
2. Instead of calculating specific percentages (another difficult concept), we make comparisons to certain "benchmark" percentages, such as 10%.

In this unit, we include an optional lesson that uses 10% as a standard of closeness for estimates. We consider an estimate to be close if it is within 10% of the desired result. Students can apply this standard to the *Spreading Out* lab and in subsequent laboratory experiments, when appropriate. They determine whether collected data falls within a reasonable range by finding if the data for individual trials falls within 10% of the median value. Keep in mind that the 10% standard is arbitrary; we use it because it is easy to calculate and for many experiments, 10% error is about the accuracy we can expect with simple equipment. There are times, however, when we can and should expect greater accuracy. For example, 10% accuracy may not be sufficient if you are trying to determine whether a piece of furniture will fit through a doorway.

For more information on estimation and accuracy, refer to the TIMS Tutor: *Estimation, Accuracy, and Error* in the *Teacher Implementation Guide.*

Resources

- Hiebert, James. "The Role of Routine Procedures in the Development of Mathematical Competence." In *Teaching and Learning Mathematics in the 1990s, 1990 Yearbook,* eds. T.J. Cooney and C.R. Hirsch, pp. 31–40. National Council of Teachers of Mathematics, Reston, VA, 1990.
- Hiebert, James. "Relationships Between Research and the NCTM Standards." *Journal for Research in Mathematics Education,* 30(1), pp. 3–19, 1999.
- van Engen, Henry, and Glenadine E. Gibb. *General Mental Functions Associated with Division,* Iowa State Teachers College, Cedar Falls, IA, 1956.

Observational Assessment Record

(A1) Can students measure area?

(A2) Can students find the median and mean of a data set?

(A3) Can students divide with 1-digit divisors using paper and pencil?

(A4) Can students estimate quotients?

(A5) Can students interpret remainders?

(A6) Can students divide numbers with ending zeros mentally?

(A7) Can students draw and interpret best-fit lines?

(A8) Can students collect, organize, graph, and analyze data?

(A9) Do students demonstrate fluency with the multiplication and division facts for the square numbers?

(A10) _____

Name	A1	A2	A3	A4	A5	A6	A7	A8	A9	A10	Comments
1.											
2.											
3.											
4.											
5.											
6.											
7.											
8.											
9.											
10.											
11.											
12.											
13.											

Name	A1	A2	A3	A4	A5	A6	A7	A8	A9	A10	Comments
14.											
15.											
16.											
17.											
18.											
19.											
20.											
21.											
22.											
23.											
24.											
25.											
26.											
27.											
28.											
29.											
30.											
31.											
32.											

Daily Practice and Problems
Division and Data

A DPP Menu for Unit 4

Two Daily Practice and Problems (DPP) items are included for each class session listed in the Unit Outline. A scope and sequence chart for the DPP is in the *Teacher Implementation Guide*.

Icons in the Teacher Notes column designate the subject matter of each DPP item. The first item in each class session is always a Bit and the second is either a Task or Challenge. Each item falls into one or more of the categories listed below. A menu of the DPP items for Unit 4 follows.

N Number Sense	Computation	Time	Geometry
C, G, H, L, N–V, X, Y, BB	A, F, G, O, P, R–U, X, Z	J	D, W
Math Facts	$ Money	Measurement	Data
B, E, I, K, M, S, Z, AA	P	A, D, F, W	T, V, Y, BB

Refer to the *Daily Practice and Problems and Home Practice Guide* in the *Teacher Implementation Guide* for further information on the DPP. The guide includes information on how and when to use the DPP.

Review and Assessment of Math Facts

By the end of fourth grade, students in *Math Trailblazers* are expected to demonstrate fluency with the multiplication and division facts. The DPP for this unit continues the systematic, strategies-based approach to reviewing the multiplication and the division facts. This unit reviews the third group of facts, the square numbers (2×2, 3×3, 4×4, etc.). The *Triangle Flash Cards* for these facts follow the Home Practice for this unit in the *Discovery Assignment Book*. Blackline masters of all the cards, organized by group, are in the *Grade 5 Facts Resource Guide*.

The following describes how the facts for the square numbers will be practiced and assessed in the DPP for this unit.

1. DPP item B instructs students to quiz each other on the facts for the square numbers using the *Triangle Flash Cards*. Students sort the cards into three piles: those facts they know and can answer quickly, those they can figure out with a strategy, and those they need to learn. The DPP item also reminds students to update their *Facts I Know* charts, which they began in Lesson 2 of Unit 2.

2. DPP item E helps students practice the multiplication facts for the square numbers. DPP items I, K, and M use fact families to introduce the related division facts. Note that the fact families for the square numbers have only two number sentences (e.g., $4 \times 4 = 16$ and $16 \div 4 = 4$). (Item S also provides more practice with the division facts for the square numbers.)

3. DPP item AA assesses students on a mixture of multiplication and division facts. Students update both their *Multiplication* and *Division Facts I Know* charts.

Note: Part 1 of the Home Practice in the *Discovery Assignment Book* reminds students to take home their flash cards to practice the facts with a family member.

For more information about the distribution and assessment of the math facts, see the TIMS Tutor: *Math Facts* in the *Teacher Implementation Guide*. Also refer to the *Grade 5 Facts Resource Guide*.

Unit ④ Daily Practice and Problems

Students may solve the items individually, in groups, or as a class. The items may also be assigned for homework. The DPPs are also available on the Teacher Resource CD.

Student Questions	Teacher Notes

 A **What's My Length?**

Here are several units of length that you should know.

12 inches (in) = 1 foot (ft)

1760 yards (yds) = 1 mile (mi)

3 feet = 1 yard

5280 feet = 1 mile

Complete the following, using the information above. Use your calculator to help you.

A. 5 ft = _____ in

B. 36 in = _____ ft

C. 27 ft = _____ yds

D. 3520 yds = _____ mi

E. 4 yds = _____ ft

F. 3 mi = _____ ft

TIMS Bit

Ask students to explain how they derived their answers.

A. 60 in
B. 3 ft
C. 9 yds
D. 2 mi
E. 12 ft
F. 15,840 ft

Multiplication and Division Facts: Square Numbers

With a partner, use your *Triangle Flash Cards* to quiz each other on the multiplication and division facts for the square numbers. Follow the directions in the *Student Guide* for Unit 2 Lesson 2 *Facts I Know.*

As your partner quizzes you on the multiplication facts, separate the facts into three piles: those facts you know and can answer quickly, those you can figure out with a strategy, and those you need to learn. Practice any facts for the square numbers in the last two piles. List these facts so you can practice them at home. Repeat the process for the division facts.

Circle all the facts you know and can answer quickly on your *Multiplication* and *Division Facts I Know* charts. As you circle the facts for the square numbers on your chart, what patterns do you see?

TIMS Task

The *Triangle Flash Cards: Square Numbers* are in the *Discovery Assignment Book* following the Home Practice. Blackline masters of all the flash cards, organized by group, are in the *Grade 5 Facts Resource Guide.* Part 1 of the Home Practice reminds students to take home the list of square numbers they need to study as well as their flash cards.

The *Multiplication* and *Division Facts I Know* charts were distributed in Unit 2 Lesson 2. As students fill in their charts, they should see that the products for the square numbers lie on the diagonal that divides the chart in half. Point out to students that they need to circle only one fact since the turn-around fact is the same.

Inform students when you will give the quiz on these facts. The quiz appears in DPP item AA.

C **Equivalent Fractions**

Complete the number sentences with the correct value for *n*.

A. $\frac{4}{8} = \frac{n}{2}$

B. $\frac{2}{3} = \frac{6}{n}$

C. $\frac{12}{9} = \frac{n}{3}$

D. $\frac{5}{12} = \frac{10}{n}$

E. $\frac{20}{16} = \frac{5}{n}$

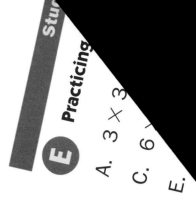

D **Area of Shapes**

Find the area of the shapes below. You may use tools such as centimeter rulers or *Centimeter Grid Paper.* Be ready to share your strategies with the class.

1.

2.

3.

TIMS Task

1. 16 sq cm

2. 24 sq cm

3. 7 sq cm

Students can measure the length and width of the square and the rectangle. Multiplying the length by the width will give the area of each. Tracing the figures on grid paper and counting square centimeters is another strategy. The legs of the triangle measure 7 cm and 2 cm. By tracing the figure on *Centimeter Grid Paper* and counting square centimeters, they can find the area of 7 sq cm. Some students may notice that the triangle is one-half of a 7 cm by 2 cm rectangle. Therefore, its area is 7 sq cm ($\frac{1}{2}$ of 14 sq cm).

Use this item to assess students' ability to find areas. Ask students to write their solution strategies along with their answers.

They can use the Student Rubric: *Telling* (see inside back cover or Appendix C of the *Student Guide*) to help them complete their answers. Use the Telling dimension of the *TIMS Multidimensional Rubric* to assist in scoring the students' work.

...the Facts

B. $8 \times 8 =$

D. $5 \times 5 =$

10 × 10 =   F. $2 \times 2 =$

G. $4 \times 4 =$ H. $7 \times 7 =$

I. $9 \times 9 =$

A. 9   B. 64

C. 36   D. 25

E. 100   F. 4

G. 16   H. 49

I. 81

F Counting Square Units

In solving the following problems, it may help to use the sketch of a square foot shown here:

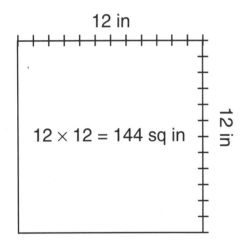

12 in

12 in

$12 \times 12 = 144$ sq in

1. How many square inches are there in two square feet?

2. How many square inches are there in one square yard?

3. How many square millimeters are there in one square meter? (1 m = 1000 mm)

TIMS Task

1. Since there are 144 square inches in 1 square foot, there are 288 square inches in 2 square feet.

2. A square yard is 3 feet by 3 feet or 36 inches by 36 inches. 36 × 36 = 1296 square inches. Or, 9 square feet × 144 sq inches = 1296 square inches.

3. 1000 mm × 1000 mm = 1,000,000 sq mm

Multiplication

Solve the following problems using a paper-and-pencil method. Estimate to be sure your answers are reasonable.

A. $73 \times 3 =$

B. $65 \times 6 =$

C. $82 \times 82 =$

TIMS Bit

A. 219

B. 390

C. 6724

 Fractions Between 0 and 1

1. Name at least one fraction between $\frac{1}{2}$ and 1.

2. Name at least one fraction between $\frac{1}{4}$ and $\frac{3}{4}$.

3. Name at least one fraction between 0 and $\frac{1}{2}$ with a denominator of 10.

4. Name at least one fraction between $\frac{7}{8}$ and 1.

5. Name at least one fraction between 0 and $\frac{1}{2}$ with a numerator that is not 1.

TIMS Task

Answers will vary. Encourage students to use the Number Lines for Fractohoppers chart in the *Student Guide* for Unit 3 Lesson 4. Here are a few possible answers:

1. $\frac{2}{3}, \frac{3}{4}, \frac{5}{6}, \frac{7}{8}, \frac{8}{9}$, etc.

2. $\frac{2}{4}, \frac{1}{2}, \frac{1}{3}, \frac{2}{3}$, etc.

3. $\frac{1}{10}, \frac{2}{10}, \frac{3}{10}, \frac{4}{10}$

4. $\frac{9}{10}, \frac{11}{12}, \frac{15}{16}$, etc.

5. $\frac{2}{6}, \frac{2}{8}, \frac{3}{7}, \frac{3}{8}, \frac{4}{16}$, etc.

Fact Families for the Square Numbers

The square numbers only have two facts in each fact family.

For example, the following two facts are in the same fact family.

$$2 \times 2 = 4 \text{ and } 4 \div 2 = 2$$

Solve the fact. Then name the second fact in the same fact family.

A. $9 \times 9 = ?$ B. $5 \times 5 = ?$

C. $7 \times 7 = ?$ D. $8 \times 8 = ?$

E. $10 \times 10 = ?$ F. $3 \times 3 = ?$

G. $6 \times 6 = ?$ H. $4 \times 4 = ?$

TIMS Bit

A. $81; 81 \div 9 = 9$

B. $25; 25 \div 5 = 5$

C. $49; 49 \div 7 = 7$

D. $64; 64 \div 8 = 8$

E. $100; 100 \div 10 = 10$

F. $9; 9 \div 3 = 3$

G. $36; 36 \div 6 = 6$

H. $16; 16 \div 4 = 4$

 Time

1. Jerome is excited about going to a professional basketball game. He is counting the hours. Today is Monday. The time is 7:00 A.M. In 36 hours the basketball game begins. What day is Jerome attending the game? At what time does the game begin?

2. Shannon fell off her bicycle. She got 10 stitches in her hand. The doctor told her to keep her hand dry for 72 hours. She leaves the doctor's office at 3:30 P.M. on Wednesday. When will the 72 hours be up?

TIMS Task

1. 7:00 P.M. on Tuesday

2. Saturday at 3:30 P.M.

Student Questions	Teacher Notes

 Fact Families for × and ÷

Complete the number sentences for the related facts.

A. $2 \times 2 =$ ___

   ___ $\div\ 2 =$ ___

B. $8 \times 8 =$ ___

   ___ $\div$ ___ $= 8$

C. $36 \div 6 =$ ___

   ___ $\times\ 6 =$ ___

D. $10 \times$ ___ $= 100$

   $100 \div$ ___ $=$ ___

TIMS Bit

A. 4; $4 \div 2 = 2$

B. 64; $64 \div 8 = 8$

C. 6; $6 \times 6 = 36$

D. 10; $100 \div 10 = 10$

 Which Is Greater?

For each pair of numbers, tell which is greater. Show how you know.

A. 3×10^4 or 7×10^2?

B. 2×10^2 or 20,000?

C. 79,300,000 or 7.93×10^5?

D. $40,000,000,000 \times 5$ or 2×10^9?

E. 3.2×10^{11} or thirty-two trillion?

TIMS Challenge

A. $30,000 > 700$

B. $200 < 20,000$

C. $7.93 \times 10^7 >$
   7.93×10^5

D. 200,000,000,000 >
   2,000,000,000

E. 320,000,000,000 <
   32,000,000,000,000

Student Questions	Teacher Notes

M Fact Families for × and ÷

Complete the number sentences for the related facts.

A. $3 \times 3 =$ ___

___ $\div 3 =$ ___

B. $7 \times 7 =$ ___

___ $\div 7 =$ ___

C. $9 \times 9 =$ ___

___ $\div 9 =$ ___

D. $25 \div 5 =$ ___

___ $\times 5 =$ ___

E. $4 \times 4 =$ ___

___ $\div$ ___ $= 4$

TIMS Bit

A. 9; $9 \div 3 = 3$

B. 49; $49 \div 7 = 7$

C. 81; $81 \div 9 = 9$

D. 5; $5 \times 5 = 25$

E. 16; $16 \div 4 = 4$

N Fractions

1. The two squares shown here together represent $\frac{1}{4}$.

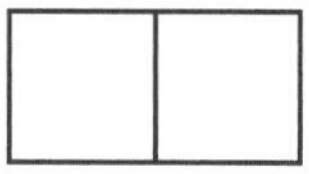

A. Draw one whole.

B. Write a fraction for one of the two squares shown above.

2. If the shape below represents $\frac{1}{6}$, show $\frac{1}{2}$.

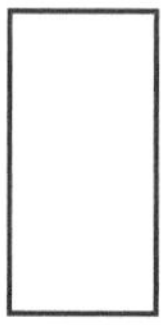

TIMS Task

1. A. Shapes will vary. One example is shown here.

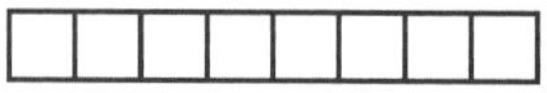

B. $\frac{1}{8}$

2.

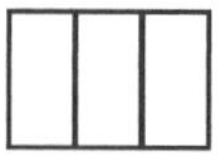

Student Questions	Teacher Notes

Shortcut Division

Use a paper-and-pencil method to solve the following problems. Estimate to make sure your answers are reasonable.

- A. 1739 ÷ 5
- B. 467 ÷ 3
- C. 1056 ÷ 6

TIMS Bit

A. 347 R4

B. 155 R2

C. 176

P Vacation Planning

Arti's grandparents are planning a three-day vacation weekend to celebrate their 40th wedding anniversary. Here is a list of things they must consider when planning how much money they will need.

- They are staying at a hotel that includes breakfast and lunch for two for a total cost of $97 each night. They are staying at the hotel for three nights.

- They plan on tipping the maid 10% of the cost of the room for one night.

- They have to buy dinner for the three evenings for $13.95 a person.

- They plan on leaving a 20% tip at the restaurant each evening.

About how much money do they need to pay for this weekend get-away? Show all the steps in your solution.

TIMS Challenge

Answers will vary slightly.

Hotel: $300
Tip for maid: about $10
Dinner: about $90
Tip at restaurant: Between $5 and $6 each evening for a total of $15–$18.
Total cost: about $418

This item is appropriate for students who have completed optional Lesson 4 *How Close Is Close Enough?*

Student Questions	Teacher Notes

 Reading Scientific Notation

Shannon solves a problem on her calculator. The answer to the problem is 6.2×10^9.

1. Write the answer in standard form.

2. Write the answer in words.

TIMS Bit

1. 6,200,000,000

2. six billion, two hundred million

 Estimation

Estimate the answers to the following problems. Then explain your thinking.

1. About how many 14s are in 150?

2. About how many 25s are in 280?

3. About how many 20s are in 312?

4. About how many 40s are in 2591?

TIMS Task

Answers will vary but should include students' strategies. Sharing these strategies with the class, or in groups, will allow students to see several ways to make estimates.

1. 10 is an example of a good estimate. $14 \times 10 = 140$

2. 10, 11, or 12; $25 \times 10 = 250$; 25×11 is the same as $25 \times 10 + 25$ or 275; Alternatively, there are four 25s in 100 and there are almost three 100s, so there are about, or slightly less than, twelve 25s.

3. $20 \times 20 = 400$ which is too high; $20 \times 10 = 200$ which is too low; 15 is an example of a good estimate.

4. 40×60 is 2400 and 40×70 is 2800; 65 is a good estimate.

Multiplying and Dividing by Multiples of 10

A. $800 \times 80 =$ B. $25{,}000 \div 50 =$

C. $4900 \div 7 =$ D. $10{,}000 \div 10 =$

E. $40 \times 400 =$ F. $8100 \div 90 =$

TIMS Bit

A. 64,000
B. 500
C. 700
D. 1000
E. 16,000
F. 90

 Within 10%?

Jerome, Lin, Nicholas, and Alexis each estimate the number of marshmallows in a jar. Jerome's estimate is 131. Lin's estimate is 120. Nicholas's estimate is 100. Alexis estimates there are 135 marshmallows in the jar. The jar actually contains 111 marshmallows. Which estimates are within 10% of 111? How do you know?

TIMS Challenge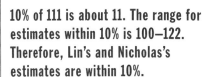

10% of 111 is about 11. The range for estimates within 10% is 100–122. Therefore, Lin's and Nicholas's estimates are within 10%.

Assign this item only to those students who have completed optional Lesson 4 *How Close Is Close Enough?*

 More Shortcut Division

Use a paper-and-pencil method to solve the following problems. Estimate to make sure your answers are reasonable.

A. $3315 \div 6 =$

B. $927 \div 7 =$

C. $3476 \div 4 =$

TIMS Bit

A. 552 R3
B. 132 R3
C. 869

and 4 drops of liquid on the same brand of paper ed the area of each spot formed. His data are shown below.

N Number of Drops	A Area (sq cm)
1	7
2	15
4	28

1. Graph Manny's data on a piece of *Centimeter Graph Paper.* Graph the number of drops on the horizontal axis and the area on the vertical axis.

2. If Manny put 6 drops of liquid on the paper towel, predict the approximate area of the new spot.

3. Write three equal ratios, in the form of a fraction, for the ratio of the area to the number of drops. Use ratios from your graph.

TIMS Task

1.

Spreading Out graph, Area (sq cm) vs N Number of Drops

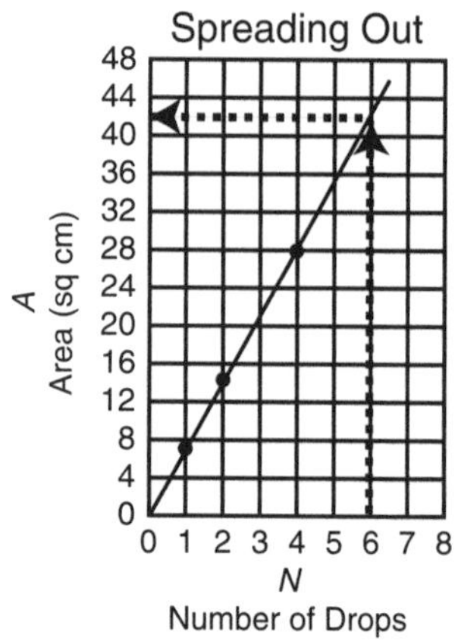

2. About 42 sq cm

3. Answers will vary.

$$\frac{21 \text{ sq cm}}{3 \text{ drops}} = \frac{28 \text{ sq cm}}{4 \text{ drops}} = \frac{35 \text{ sq cm}}{5 \text{ drops}}$$

Decorating the House

Jackie wants to cut rectangles from material to make rugs for her miniature doll house. She measures the living room and family room floors. Her measurements are listed below. Find the area of the floor in each of these rooms.

Living room: 7 cm by 9 cm

Family room: 7 cm by 11 cm

TIMS Bit

Living room: 63 sq cm

Family room: 77 sq cm

X **What's That Number?**

Find a number between 200 and 300 that is divisible by 2, 3, and 5. What strategies did you use?

TIMS Challenge

210, 240, and 270

Strategies might include knowing the number must be even to be divisible by 2 or must end in a 0 to be divisible by 2 and 5.

Y Medians and Means

In Language Arts, the students in Mr. Moreno's class are reading a novel together. Their homework each night is to continue reading the book. Every Monday each student reports the number of pages he or she read the week before. Jackie's data are shown below.

Day of the Week	Number of Pages
Monday	15
Tuesday	3
Wednesday	5
Thursday	7
Friday	20

1. What is the median number of pages Jackie read?

2. What is the mean number of pages Jackie read?

3. Which average would you use to represent the data? Why?

TIMS Bit

1. 7 pages

2. 10 pages

3. Answers will vary. Some students may choose the mean since it includes 20 pages and 15 pages in the calculation. The higher number will "pull up" the average. Other students may choose the median since it is easy to calculate.

| Student Questions | Teacher Notes |

 Z **Order of Operations**

Solve each pair of problems and compare their answers.

A. $5 \times (7 - 2) =$

$5 \times 7 - 2 =$

B. $30 - 3 \times 7 =$

$(30 - 3) \times 7 =$

C. $18 \div 2 \times 3 =$

$18 \div (2 \times 3) =$

D. $(4 + 3) \times (8 + 2) =$

$4 + 3 \times 8 + 2 =$

TIMS Task

Students should see that using parentheses changes the answers.

A. 25; 33

B. 9; 189

C. 27; 3

D. 70; 30

 AA **Quiz: Square Numbers**

A. $5 \times 5 =$ B. $4 \div 2 =$

C. $81 \div 9 =$ D. $10 \times 10 =$

E. $8 \times 8 =$ F. $16 \div 4 =$

G. $9 \div 3 =$ H. $6 \times 6 =$

I. $49 \div 7 =$

TIMS Bit

We recommend 2 minutes for this quiz. Allow students to change pens after the time is up and complete the remaining problems in a different color. After students take the quiz, have them update their *Multiplication Facts I Know* and *Division Facts I Know* charts.

BB **Collecting Data**

How many sit-ups can you do in one minute? Collect data from your classmates. One student in each pair can take turns being the timekeeper. Once you collect the data, find the median and mean number of sit-ups the students in your sample can do.

TIMS Challenge

You may suggest to the P.E. teacher that he or she help students in their data collection.

Grid Area

Lesson Overview

Estimated Class Sessions

2

In this lesson, students discover and compare strategies for finding areas of geometric figures. Students then use these strategies to find areas of figures with straight sides and to estimate areas of figures with curved sides. Through examples, students generalize the formula for the area of a rectangle as length times width. Students will apply the skills learned in this lesson in the lab *Spreading Out*.

Key Content

- Using strategies to find the area of geometric figures.
- Using multiplication facts to find the area of geometric figures.
- Counting square centimeters to estimate the area of figures with curved sides.
- Generalizing the area of a rectangle as length times width.

Key Vocabulary

- area
- length
- square centimeter
- width

Math Facts

Complete DPP item B and begin reviewing the multiplication and division facts for the square numbers.

Homework

1. Assign the *Finding Area* and *Cut and Paste Puzzles* Homework Pages in the *Discovery Assignment Book.*
2. Assign the Homework section in the *Student Guide.*
3. Assign Parts 1 and 2 of the Home Practice.

Assessment

1. Use the *Observational Assessment Record* to record students' abilities to find the area of a shape.
2. Use the *Finding Area* Activity Page as an assessment.
3. Use DPP item D as a short assessment.

Curriculum Sequence

Before This Unit

Students using *Math Trailblazers* had many experiences with area in Grades K–4. In third grade, they found the area of figures with straight sides and estimated the area of figures with curved sides by counting square centimeters (see Grade 3 Unit 5). In fourth grade, students found the area and perimeter of shapes built with square-inch tiles (see Grade 4 Unit 2).

After This Unit

Students use the area of rectangles as a model for multiplying decimals in Unit 7. They use the concepts in this unit to develop a formula for the area of a triangle in Unit 15. For more information on area, see the TIMS Tutor: *Area* in the *Teacher Implementation Guide.*

Materials List

Supplies and Copies

Student	Teacher
Supplies for Each Student • ruler • scissors • glue	**Supplies**
Copies • 3–4 copies of *Centimeter Grid Paper* per student (*Unit Resource Guide* Page 44)	**Copies/Transparencies** • 1 transparency of *Centimeter Grid Paper* (*Unit Resource Guide* Page 44) • 1 transparency of *Under the Rug* (*Discovery Assignment Book* Page 53) • 1 copy of *Observational Assessment Record* to be used throughout this unit (*Unit Resource Guide* Pages 13–14)

All blackline masters including assessment, transparency, and DPP masters are also on the Teacher Resource CD.

Student Books

Grid Area (*Student Guide* Pages 102–105)
Triangle Flash Cards: Square Numbers (*Discovery Assignment Book* Pages 47–48)
Strategies to Find Area (*Discovery Assignment Book* Pages 49–50)
Finding Area (*Discovery Assignment Book* Page 51)
Under the Rug (*Discovery Assignment Book* Page 53), optional
Cut and Paste Puzzles (*Discovery Assignment Book* Pages 55–59)
Super Challenge: Cut and Paste Puzzle (*Discovery Assignment Book* Pages 61–63), optional

Daily Practice and Problems and Home Practice

DPP items A–D (*Unit Resource Guide* Pages 17–19)
Home Practice Parts 1–2 (*Discovery Assignment Book* Page 43)

Note: Classrooms whose pacing differs significantly from the suggested pacing of the units should use the Math Facts Calendar in Section 4 of the *Facts Resource Guide* to ensure students receive the complete math facts program.

Assessment Tools

Observational Assessment Record (*Unit Resource Guide* Pages 13–14)

Daily Practice and Problems

Suggestions for using the DPPs are on pages 41–42.

A. Bit: What's My Length? (URG p. 17)

Here are several units of length that you should know.

12 inches (in) = 1 foot (ft)

1760 yards (yds) = 1 mile (mi)

3 feet = 1 yard

5280 feet = 1 mile

Complete the following, using the information above. Use your calculator to help you.

  A. 5 ft = ___ in

  B. 36 in = ___ ft

  C. 27 ft = ___ yds

  D. 3520 yds = ___ mi

  E. 4 yds = ___ ft

  F. 3 mi = ___ ft

B. Task: Multiplication and Division Facts: Square Numbers (URG p. 18)

With a partner, use your *Triangle Flash Cards* to quiz each other on the multiplication and division facts for the square numbers. Follow the directions in the *Student Guide* for Unit 2 Lesson 2 *Facts I Know.*

As your partner quizzes you on the multiplication facts, separate the facts into three piles: those facts you know and can answer quickly, those you can figure out with a strategy, and those you need to learn. Practice any facts for the square numbers in the last two piles. List these facts so you can practice them at home. Repeat the process for the division facts.

Circle all the facts you know and can answer quickly on your *Multiplication* and *Division Facts I Know* charts. As you circle the facts for the square numbers on your chart, what patterns do you see?

C. Bit: Equivalent Fractions (URG p. 19)

Complete the number sentences with the correct value for *n*.

  A. $\frac{4}{8} = \frac{n}{2}$ B. $\frac{2}{3} = \frac{6}{n}$

  C. $\frac{12}{9} = \frac{n}{3}$ D. $\frac{5}{12} = \frac{10}{n}$

  E. $\frac{20}{16} = \frac{5}{n}$

D. Task: Area of Shapes (URG p. 19)

Find the area of the shapes below. You may use tools such as centimeter rulers or *Centimeter Grid Paper.* Be ready to share your strategies with the class.

  1.

  2.

  3.

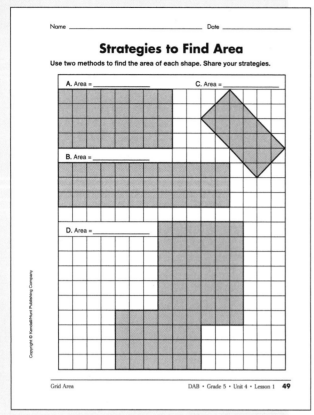

Discovery Assignment Book - page 49 *(Answers on p. 48)*

TIMS Tip

Correct students if they overgeneralize and say incorrect statements such as "area is length times width." Remind them that they are probably referring to the area of a rectangle, and not making a statement about the area of all shapes.

Content Note

There is no hard-and-fast rule for defining which side of a rectangle is the length and which is the width. We simply call one side the **length,** and an adjacent side the **width.**

Teaching the Activity

This activity has two parts. Student pages for the first part are in the *Discovery Assignment Book.* Student pages for the second part are in the *Student Guide.*

Part 1   Strategies to Find Area

Have students share their understanding of area and discuss times when it is important to know how to determine area. Talk about the different units that people use to measure area.

Use the *Strategies to Find Area* Activity Pages in the *Discovery Assignment Book* as discussion pages. Students may work together in small groups or as a class to discuss the various strategies they can use to find the areas of the figures.

Since Figure A on the *Strategies to Find Area* Activity Pages is a 4 cm × 8 cm rectangle composed of whole squares, students can find the area of 32 square centimeters by counting. A more sophisticated strategy is to note that there are 4 rows of 8 sq cm each (or 8 columns of 4 sq cm each) and they can multiply or skip count to get 32 sq cm. They can use similar strategies to find the area of Figure B. Discuss the positive and negative aspects of each strategy. Ask students:

- *What is the area of a rectangle that has 5 rows of 8 centimeter squares?*

Students should respond that the area is 40 sq cm. Explain to students that we can also look at this as a rectangle whose dimensions are 5 cm by 8 cm. Illustrate this on the board or overhead. (5 cm × 8 cm = 40 sq cm.) Ask questions such as:

- *What is the area of a rectangle whose dimensions are 10 cm by 6 cm?*
- *What is the area of a rectangle whose dimensions are 5 inches by 7 inches?*
- *What is the area of an 8 m by 9 m rectangle?*
- *What is the area of a square whose sides are 7 cm?*

If students are uncertain, sketch the rectangles for them. Students should use the correct units when giving answers. Remind students that a square is a rectangle. Thus the area of the square with 7-cm sides is 49 sq cm. Generalize that the area of a rectangle is the length times the width.

While Figure C is still a rectangle, students should notice that it is not made up entirely of whole centimeter squares. This figure has several centimeter squares that are cut in half. Use a transparency of *Centimeter Grid Paper* and review how to combine two half-squares to make one whole centimeter square when finding the area. Figure C contains 10 whole centimeter squares and 12 half-squares.

The total area is 16 square centimeters. Ask students how they can find the area of Figure C using multiplication. Encourage them to measure each side to the nearest tenth of a centimeter and then multiply length by width on their calculators—5.7 cm × 2.8 cm = 15.96 sq cm or 16 sq cm to the nearest sq cm. Remind students that since we cannot measure the length of a side exactly, the answer on the calculator will not be the exact area.

One possible strategy to find the area of Figure D is to divide this large shape into several smaller rectangles. Count each smaller rectangle and then add the areas together to arrive at the total area of 63 sq cm. Another possible strategy is to draw the rectangle that surrounds this shape and find its area (90 sq cm) as shown in Figure 7. Then find the area of the two unshaded rectangles (18 sq cm and 9 sq cm). Then subtract the total from 90 sq cm to find the area of the shaded shape.

Finding the Area of a Triangle. After counting the area of both Figures E and F, ask students if they notice any similarities in the two shapes. The triangle is half the area of the rectangle; fold a copy of the rectangle to illustrate this. The height of the triangle is equal to the length of the rectangle and the base of the triangle is equal to the width of the rectangle. We do not intend to develop the formula for the area of a triangle here, but rather slowly build intuitive understanding. One possible strategy to find the area of the triangle is to draw the rectangle that surrounds the triangle and find its area. Divide this in half to find the area of the triangle.

Shapes with Curved Sides. In the final problem in this activity, students estimate the area of shapes with curved sides. Students who did not use *Math Trailblazers* in third grade may not have had prior experience with this and may need some practice. Trace Figure G on the transparency of *Centimeter Grid Paper*. Ask students how they can estimate the area of the figure. Use your drawing to demonstrate how to first count whole square units in the shape. Then look for fractional units to combine with one another to make a whole unit. All these are added together to estimate the total area. Two methods for

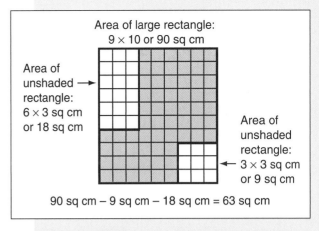

Figure 7: *Finding the area of Figure D by drawing a rectangle around the entire figure*

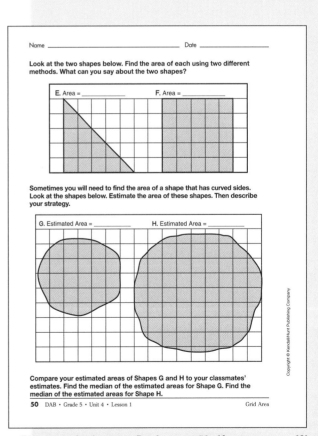

Discovery Assignment Book - page 50 (Answers on p. 49)

finding the area of Figure G are shown in Figure 8. The area is approximately 24 sq cm. Note: We numbered the fractional units to indicate how they combine to make whole units. For example, the pieces labeled 17 combine to make the seventeenth whole unit.

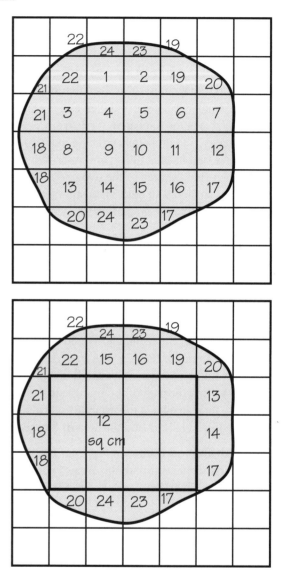

Figure 8: *Two methods for estimating the area of a figure with curved sides by counting sq cm*

After demonstrating this strategy on the overhead, give students time to practice estimating the area of Figure H. The area of Figure H is approximately 59 or 60 sq cm. One alternative strategy is to draw a rectangle that surrounds the shape. Then estimate the number of square centimeters that are not shaded and subtract this number from the area of the rectangle.

You can use the *Finding Area* Activity Page in the *Discovery Assignment Book* as homework or assessment after Part 1 of this lesson. You can also assign the *Cut and Paste Puzzles* Homework Pages in the *Discovery Assignment Book* as homework after Parts 1 or 2.

Part 2 More Strategies to Find Area

Begin Part 2 by discussing the ways students found area on the *Finding Area* Homework Page.

The *Grid Area* Activity Pages in the *Student Guide* lead students to other strategies for finding area. The diagrams used are more difficult as the grid lines are removed from the inside of the shape. Finally, students are presented with a shape that has no grid lines. A ruler will be needed to find the area of these shapes.

Discuss the *Student Guide* pages together as a class, allowing students time to work on problems individually or in groups. Students may use the *Under the Rug* Activity Page from the *Discovery Assignment Book* to draw in the grid lines for Figures C and D that are on the *Student Guide* pages. Use a transparency of the page to demonstrate on the overhead.

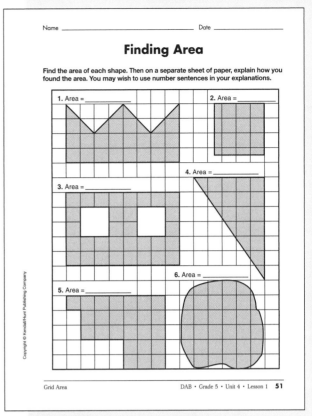

Discovery Assignment Book - page 51 (Answers on p. 49)

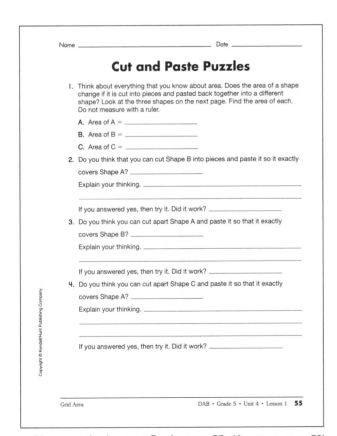

Discovery Assignment Book - page 55 (Answers on p. 50)

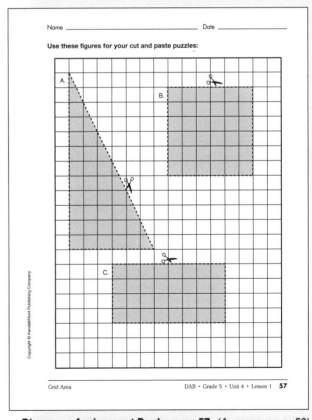

Discovery Assignment Book - page 57 (Answers on p. 50)

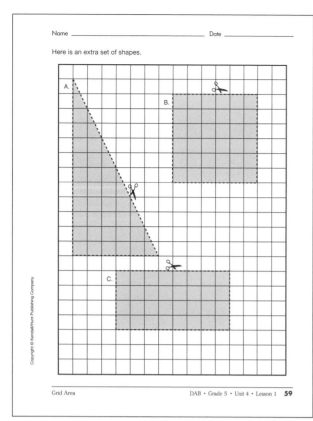

Discovery Assignment Guide - page 59 *(Answers on p. 50)*

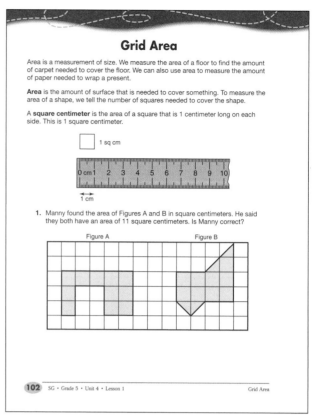

Student Guide - page 102 *(Answers on p. 45)*

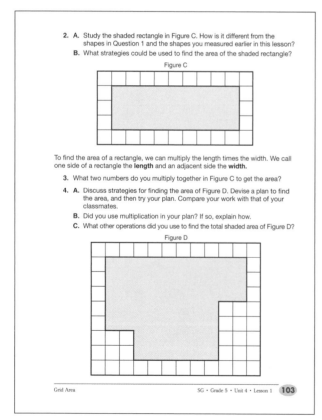

Student Guide - page 103 *(Answers on p. 45)*

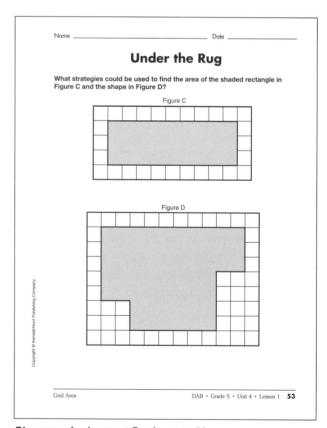

Discovery Assignment Book - page 53

In **Question 5** students should notice that one-half of the rectangle is shaded. The area of the rectangle is 27 sq cm. Since the triangle is one half of this area, divide by 2 and get $13\frac{1}{2}$ sq cm for the area of the triangle.

Students should see that a ruler is needed to find the area in **Question 7.** The area of the rectangle in sq cm is 7 cm $\times$ 5 cm or 35 sq cm. Students will also need rulers to draw the shapes in **Question 8.**

Journal Prompt

Explain two methods for finding the area of a rectangle. Show why the two methods both give the correct answer.

Math Facts

DPP item B introduces the multiplication and division facts for the square numbers.

Homework and Practice

- You can use the *Finding Area* Activity Page in the *Discovery Assignment Book* as homework after Part 1 of this lesson.

- You can also assign the *Cut and Paste Puzzles* Homework Pages in the *Discovery Assignment Book* as homework after Parts 1 or 2. Two copies of Shapes A, B, and C are provided on the *Cut and Paste Puzzles* Homework Pages to complete the task. These problems will allow students the opportunity for independent practice using the strategies developed in Part 1. The problems help illustrate that cutting a figure apart and gluing it into a different shape does not change its area. Shapes A and B have the same area (36 sq cm) so they can be cut to fit on top of one another.

- Use the Homework section on the *Grid Area* Activity Pages in the *Student Guide* after Part 2.

- Assign DPP Bits A and C, which review measurement and fractions.

- Assign Parts 1 and 2 of the Home Practice, which review math facts and area.

Answers for Parts 1 and 2 of the Home Practice are in the Answer Key at the end of this lesson and at the end of this unit.

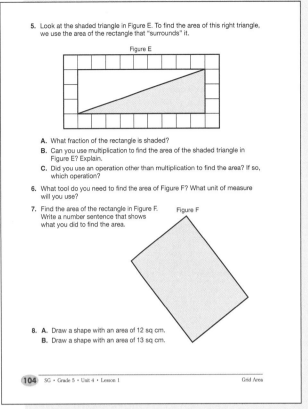

5. Look at the shaded triangle in Figure E. To find the area of this right triangle, we use the area of the rectangle that "surrounds" it.

Figure E

A. What fraction of the rectangle is shaded?
B. Can you use multiplication to find the area of the shaded triangle in Figure E? Explain.
C. Did you use an operation other than multiplication to find the area? If so, which operation?

6. What tool do you need to find the area of Figure F? What unit of measure will you use?

7. Find the area of the rectangle in Figure F. Write a number sentence that shows what you did to find the area.

Figure F

8. A. Draw a shape with an area of 12 sq cm.
B. Draw a shape with an area of 13 sq cm.

Student Guide - page 104 *(Answers on p. 46)*

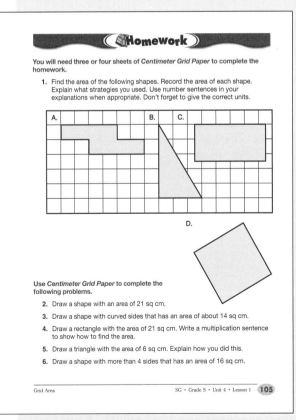

Homework

You will need three or four sheets of *Centimeter Grid Paper* to complete the homework.

1. Find the area of the following shapes. Record the area of each shape. Explain what strategies you used. Use number sentences in your explanations when appropriate. Don't forget to give the correct units.

A.   B.   C.

D.

Use *Centimeter Grid Paper* to complete the following problems.

2. Draw a shape with an area of 21 sq cm.
3. Draw a shape with curved sides that has an area of about 14 sq cm.
4. Draw a rectangle with the area of 21 sq cm. Write a multiplication sentence to show how to find the area.
5. Draw a triangle with the area of 6 sq cm. Explain how you did this.
6. Draw a shape with more than 4 sides that has an area of 16 sq cm.

Student Guide - page 105 *(Answers on p. 47)*

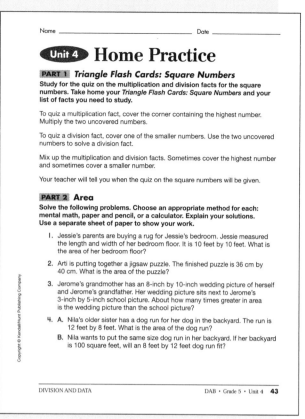

Discovery Assignment Book - page 43 *(Answers on p. 48)*

- Use the *Observational Assessment Record* to record students' abilities to find the area of a shape.

- You can use the *Finding Area* Activity Page in the *Discovery Assignment Book* as an assessment page.

- Use DPP item D to assess students' ability to find the area of rectangles and other shapes.

- Use students' responses to the Journal Prompt to assess whether students can find the area of a rectangle.

Extension

You can use the *Super Challenge: Cut and Paste Puzzle* Activity Pages in the *Discovery Assignment Book* as an extension activity for those students who complete their work early or who desire an extra challenge.

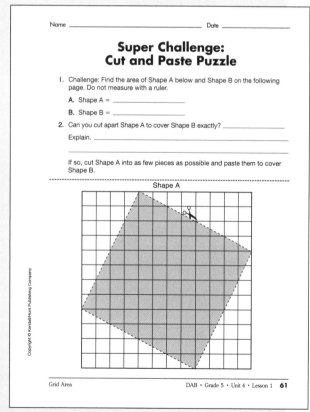

Discovery Assignment Book - page 61 *(Answers on p. 51)*

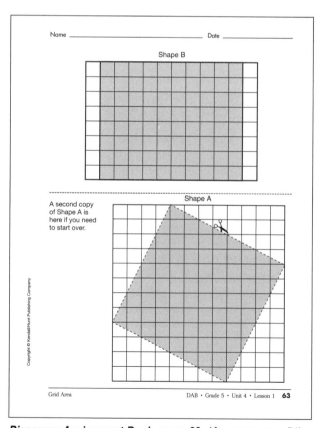

Discovery Assignment Book - page 63 *(Answers on p. 51)*

Estimated Class Sessions

2

At a Glance

Math Facts and Daily Practice and Problems
Complete DPP items A–D and begin reviewing the multiplication and division facts for the square numbers.

Part 1. Strategies to Find Area
1. Lead students in a discussion defining area and finding examples where area is used in real life.
2. Students review strategies for finding the area of figures with straight sides using a grid. Use the *Strategies to Find Area* Activity Pages in the *Discovery Assignment Book* to guide the discussion.
3. Develop the formula for finding the area of a rectangle: length × width = area.
4. Students review strategies for finding the area of figures on grids that include fractions of square centimeters.
5. Students develop strategies for estimating the area of figures with curved sides.

Part 2. More Strategies to Find Area
1. Review strategies students used while completing the *Strategies to Find Area* Activity Pages in the *Discovery Assignment Book*. Go over the previous night's homework.
2. Students develop strategies for finding the area of figures without grid lines inside. Use the *Grid Area* Activity Pages in the *Student Guide* as well as the *Under the Rug* Activity Page in the *Discovery Assignment Book* to guide the discussion.
3. Assign the *Super Challenge: Cut and Paste Puzzle* Activity Pages in the *Discovery Assignment Book* as an extension.

Homework
1. Assign the *Finding Area* and *Cut and Paste Puzzles* Homework Pages in the *Discovery Assignment Book*.
2. Assign the Homework section in the *Student Guide*.
3. Assign Parts 1 and 2 of the Home Practice.

Assessment
1. Use the *Observational Assessment Record* to record students' abilities to find the area of a shape.
2. Use the *Finding Area* Activity Page as an assessment.
3. Use DPP item D as a short assessment.

Extension
Assign the *Super Challenge: Cut and Paste Puzzle* Activity Page.

Answer Key is on pages 45–51.

Notes:

Centimeter Grid Paper

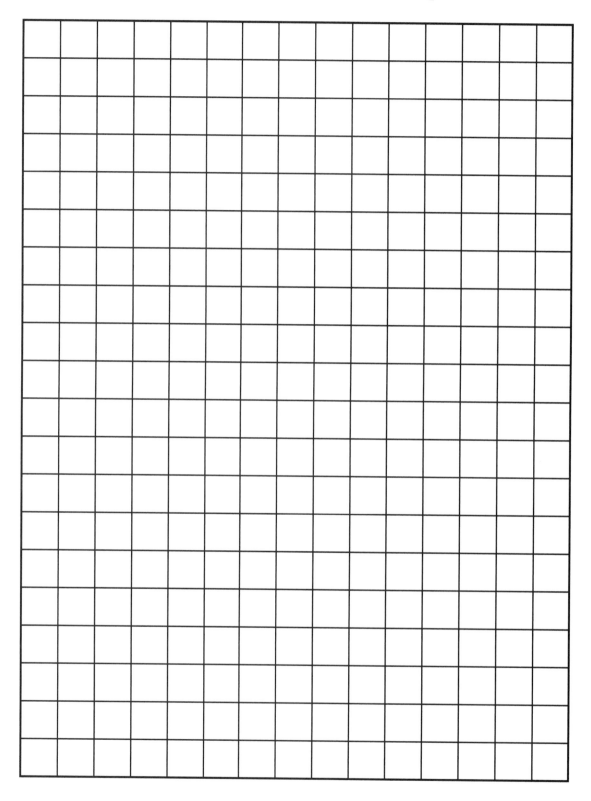

Student Guide (pp. 102–103)

1. Yes

2. **A.** The figure does not have an interior grid.

   B. Answers will vary. Students could place a transparent grid on the figure, they could measure the side lengths of the rectangle and multiply, or they could draw in the grid lines and count square centimeters.

3. 9 and 3—the length and width of the rectangle.

4. **A.–C.** Answers will vary. The area of Figure D is 58 sq cm.

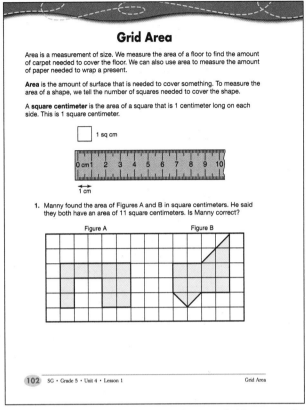

Student Guide - page 102

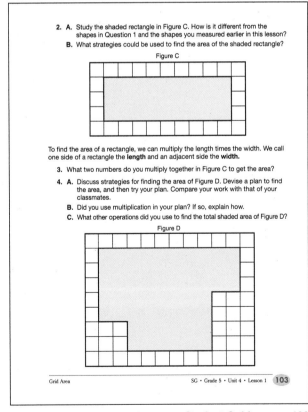

Student Guide - page 103

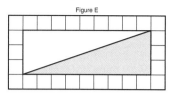

5. Look at the shaded triangle in Figure E. To find the area of this right triangle, we use the area of the rectangle that "surrounds" it.

Figure E

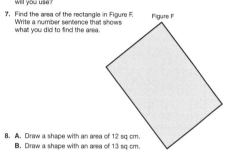

A. What fraction of the rectangle is shaded?

B. Can you use multiplication to find the area of the shaded triangle in Figure E? Explain.

C. Did you use an operation other than multiplication to find the area? If so, which operation?

6. What tool do you need to find the area of Figure F? What unit of measure will you use?

7. Find the area of the rectangle in Figure F. Write a number sentence that shows what you did to find the area.

Figure F

8. **A.** Draw a shape with an area of 12 sq cm.
   B. Draw a shape with an area of 13 sq cm.

Grid Area

Student Guide - page 104

Student Guide (p. 104)

5. **A.** one-half

   B. Yes, $9 \times 3 = 27$; $27 \div 2 = 13.5$ sq cm

   C. Yes, division.

6. ruler, centimeters (inches could be used as well)

7. $7 \text{ cm} \times 5 \text{ cm} = 35$ sq cm

8. **A.** Shapes will vary. Four possible shapes are shown below.

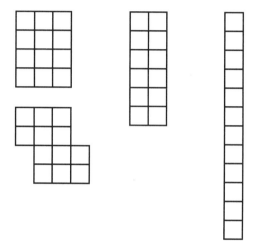

B. Shapes will vary. Two possible shapes are shown below.

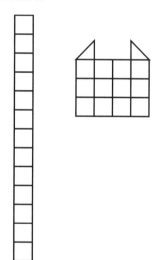

Student Guide (p. 105)

Homework

1. **A.** 8 sq cm. Strategies will vary. One possible strategy is to divide the shape into several rectangles and find the area of each rectangle. 2 cm × 1 cm + 2 cm × 2 cm + 2 cm × 1 cm = 8 sq cm.

   B. 7.5 sq cm. Strategies will vary. One possible strategy is to find the area of the rectangle two of the triangles will make and divide that area in half. 5 cm × 3 cm ÷ 2 = 7.5 sq cm.

   C. 12.5 sq cm. Strategies will vary. One possible strategy is to measure the lengths of the sides. 5 cm × 2.5 cm = 12.5 sq cm.

   D. 16 sq cm. Strategies will vary. One possible strategy is to measure the lengths of the sides. 4 cm × 4 cm = 16 sq cm.

2. Shapes will vary. One possible shape is shown.

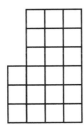

3. Shapes will vary. One possible shape is shown.

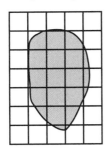

4. Rectangles will vary. One possible rectangle is shown. 7 cm × 3 cm = 21 sq cm

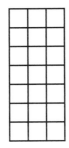

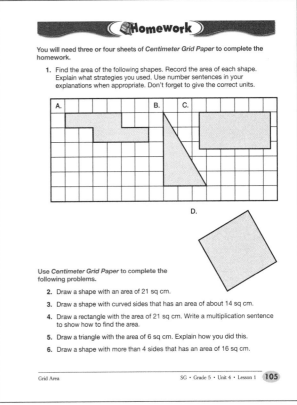

Student Guide - page 105

5. Explanations will vary. One possible solution is shown where the triangle has half the area of the 12 sq cm rectangle.

6. Shapes will vary. One possible shape is shown.

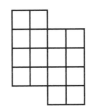

Name _____ Date _____

Unit 4 Home Practice

PART 1 *Triangle Flash Cards: Square Numbers*

Study for the quiz on the multiplication and division facts for the square numbers. Take home your *Triangle Flash Cards: Square Numbers* and your list of facts you need to study.

To quiz a multiplication fact, cover the corner containing the highest number. Multiply the two uncovered numbers.

To quiz a division fact, cover one of the smaller numbers. Use the two uncovered numbers to solve a division fact.

Mix up the multiplication and division facts. Sometimes cover the highest number and sometimes cover a smaller number.

Your teacher will tell you when the quiz on the square numbers will be given.

PART 2 Area

Solve the following problems. Choose an appropriate method for each: mental math, paper and pencil, or a calculator. Explain your solutions. Use a separate sheet of paper to show your work.

1. Jessie's parents are buying a rug for Jessie's bedroom. Jessie measured the length and width of her bedroom floor. It is 10 feet by 10 feet. What is the area of her bedroom floor?

2. Arti is putting together a jigsaw puzzle. The finished puzzle is 36 cm by 40 cm. What is the area of the puzzle?

3. Jerome's grandmother has an 8-inch by 10-inch wedding picture of herself and Jerome's grandfather. Her wedding picture sits next to Jerome's 3-inch by 5-inch school picture. About how many times greater in area is the wedding picture than the school picture?

4. A. Nila's older sister has a dog run for her dog in the backyard. The run is 12 feet by 8 feet. What is the area of the dog run?
   B. Nila wants to put the same size dog run in her backyard. If her backyard is 100 square feet, will an 8 feet by 12 feet dog run fit?

DIVISION AND DATA   DAB • Grade 5 • Unit 4   **43**

Discovery Assignment Book - page 43

Discovery Assignment Book (p. 43)

Home Practice*

Part 2. Area

1. 100 square feet
2. 1440 square centimeters
3. About 5 times greater
4. **A.** 96 square feet
   B. Yes, if the backyard is 8 feet by 12.5 feet or $8\frac{1}{3}$ feet by 12 feet.

Name _____ Date _____

Strategies to Find Area

Use two methods to find the area of each shape. Share your strategies.

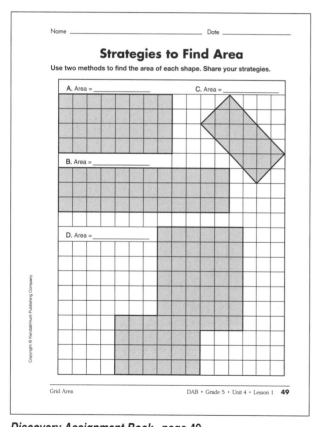

Grid Area   DAB • Grade 5 • Unit 4 • Lesson 1   **49**

Discovery Assignment Book - page 49

Discovery Assignment Book (p. 49)

Strategies to Find Area

A. 32 sq cm*

B. 36 sq cm*

C. 16 sq cm*

D. 63 sq cm*

---

*Answers for all the Home Practice in the *Discovery Assignment Book* are at the end of the unit

Discovery Assignment Book (p. 50)

E. 12.5 sq cm. The triangle has one-half the area of Shape F.*

F. 25 sq cm. The square has double the area of Shape E.*

G. About 24 sq cm. Strategies will vary. Medians will vary. See Figure 8 in Lesson Guide 1 for examples.*

H. About 60 sq cm. Strategies will vary. Medians will vary.

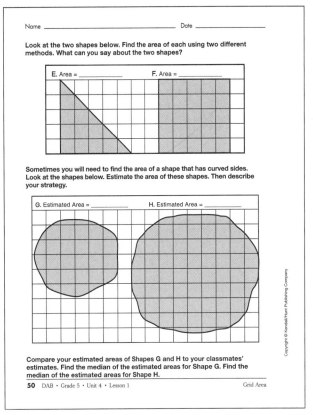

Discovery Assignment Book - page 50

Discovery Assignment Book (p. 51)

Finding Area

Explanations will vary for *Questions 1–6.*

1. 24 sq cm

2. $12\frac{1}{4}$ sq cm

3. 32 sq cm

4. $17\frac{1}{2}$ sq cm

5. 25 sq cm

6. About 30–31 sq cm

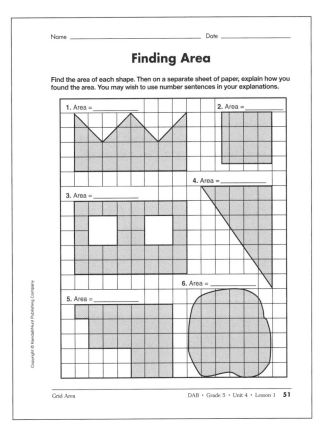

Discovery Assignment Book - page 51

*Answers for all the Home Practice in the *Discovery Assignment Book* are at the end of the unit

Name _____ Date _____

Cut and Paste Puzzles

1. Think about everything that you know about area. Does the area of a shape change if it is cut into pieces and pasted back together into a different shape? Look at the three shapes on the next page. Find the area of each. Do not measure with a ruler.

   A. Area of A = _____

   B. Area of B = _____

   C. Area of C = _____

2. Do you think that you can cut Shape B into pieces and paste it so it exactly covers Shape A? _____

   Explain your thinking. _____

   _____

   If you answered yes, then try it. Did it work? _____

3. Do you think you can cut apart Shape A and paste it so that it exactly covers Shape B? _____

   Explain your thinking. _____

   _____

   If you answered yes, then try it. Did it work? _____

4. Do you think you can cut apart Shape C and paste it so that it exactly covers Shape A? _____

   Explain your thinking. _____

   _____

   _____

   If you answered yes, then try it. Did it work? _____

Grid Area   DAB • Grade 5 • Unit 4 • Lesson 1   **55**

Discovery Assignment Book - page 55

Discovery Assignment Book (pp. 55, 57, 59)

Cut and Paste Puzzles

1. **A.** 36 sq cm

   B. 36 sq cm

   C. 32 sq cm

2. Yes. Shape A and B have the same area.

3. Yes. Shape A and B have the same area.

4. No. Shape C has an area of 32 sq cm while Shape A has an area of 36 sq cm.

Name _____ Date _____

Use these figures for your cut and paste puzzles:

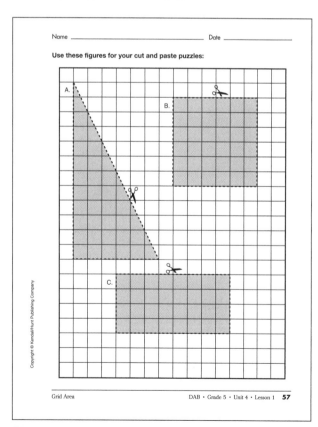

Grid Area   DAB • Grade 5 • Unit 4 • Lesson 1   **57**

Discovery Assignment Book - page 57

Name _____ Date _____

Here is an extra set of shapes.

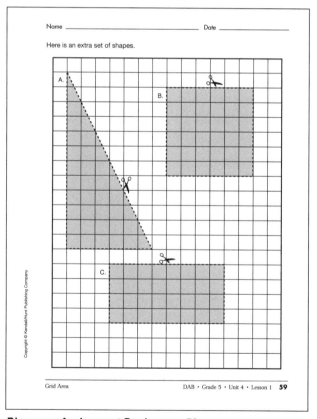

Grid Area   DAB • Grade 5 • Unit 4 • Lesson 1   **59**

Discovery Assignment Book - page 59

Discovery Assignment Book (pp. 61, 63)

Super Challenge: Cut and Paste Puzzle

1. **A.** 80 sq cm

   B. 80 sq cm

2. Yes. Shape A and Shape B have the same area. If students cut out the pieces as shown below, they will find that the areas are equivalent. (For a rough check students can measure Shape A. Its length and width are between 8.9 cm and 9 cm; $8.9 \times 8.9 = 79.2$ sq cm and $9 \times 9 = 81$ sq cm. Therefore, the area is between 79.2 and 81 sq cm.)

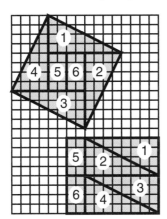

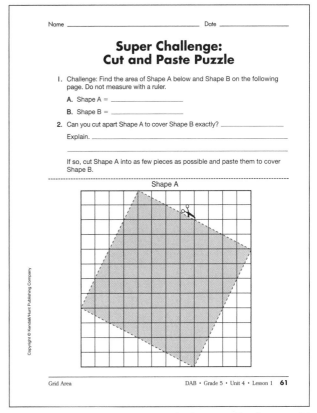

Discovery Assignment Book - page 61

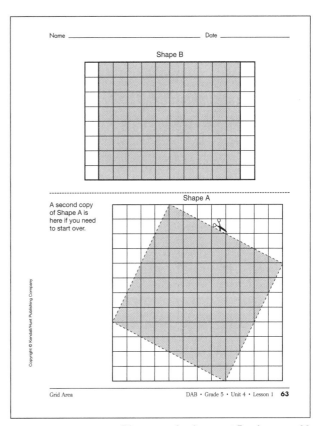

Discovery Assignment Book - page 63

Lesson 2

Modeling Division

Lesson Overview

Estimated Class Sessions

2

Base-ten pieces are used to review the concept of division. Students write related division and multiplication sentences and interpret remainders. Students build their mental division skills by looking at patterns. Estimation is stressed throughout.

Key Content

- Modeling division with base-ten pieces.
- Dividing numbers with ending zeros.
- Estimating quotients.
- Interpreting remainders.

Key Vocabulary

- dividend
- divisor
- quotient
- remainder

Math Facts

Complete item E and continue reviewing the multiplication and division facts for the square numbers.

Homework

Assign homework *Questions 1–15* in the *Student Guide*.

Assessment

Use the *Observational Assessment Record* to record students' abilities to model division with base-ten pieces.

Curriculum Sequence

Before This Unit

Division is discussed throughout the curriculum, but in particular students were introduced to a paper-and-pencil method for division in fourth grade in Unit 13.

After This Unit

Unit 9 focuses on dividing by two-digit divisors.

Materials List

Supplies and Copies

Student	Teacher
Supplies for Each Student • calculator **Supplies for Each Student Pair** • 1 set of base-ten pieces (2 packs, 14 flats, 30 skinnies, 50 bits)	**Supplies** • overhead base-ten pieces, optional
Copies • 1 table from *Multiplication Table* per student (*Unit Resource Guide* Page 61) • copies of *Base-Ten Pieces Masters* as needed (*Unit Resource Guide* Pages 62–63)	**Copies/Transparencies**

All blackline masters including assessment, transparency, and DPP masters are also on the Teacher Resource CD.

Student Books

Modeling Division (*Student Guide* Pages 106–112)

Daily Practice and Problems and Home Practice

DPP items E–H (*Unit Resource Guide* Pages 20–21)

Note: Classrooms whose pacing differs significantly from the suggested pacing of the units should use the Math Facts Calendar in Section 4 of the *Facts Resource Guide* to ensure students receive the complete math facts program.

Assessment Tools

Observational Assessment Record (*Unit Resource Guide* Pages 13–14)

Daily Practice and Problems

Suggestions for using the DPPs are on page 59.

E. Bit: Practicing the Facts (URG p. 20)

A. $3 \times 3 =$	B. $8 \times 8 =$
C. $6 \times 6 =$	D. $5 \times 5 =$
E. $10 \times 10 =$	F. $2 \times 2 =$
G. $4 \times 4 =$	H. $7 \times 7 =$
I. $9 \times 9 =$	

G. Bit: Multiplication (URG p. 21)

Solve the following problems using a paper-and-pencil method. Estimate to be sure your answers are reasonable.

A. $73 \times 3 =$	B. $65 \times 6 =$
C. $82 \times 82 =$	

F. Task: Counting Square Units
(URG p. 20)

In solving the following problems, it may help to use the sketch of a square foot shown here:

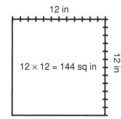

1. How many square inches are there in two square feet?

2. How many square inches are there in one square yard?

3. How many square millimeters are there in one square meter?
   ($1 \text{ m} = 1000 \text{ mm}$)

H. Task: Fractions Between 0 and 1
(URG p. 21)

1. Name at least one fraction between $\frac{1}{2}$ and 1.

2. Name at least one fraction between $\frac{1}{4}$ and $\frac{3}{4}$.

3. Name at least one fraction between 0 and $\frac{1}{2}$ with a denominator of 10.

4. Name at least one fraction between $\frac{7}{8}$ and 1.

5. Name at least one fraction between 0 and $\frac{1}{2}$ with a numerator that is not 1.

In Part 1 of the activity, students use base-ten pieces to model division problems that do not contain remainders. Part 2 focuses on problems with remainders.

Part 1 **Interpreting Division**

Distribute the base-ten pieces and begin class with the following problem:

On Monday morning, Mr. Moreno's odometer read 67,236 miles. Mr. Moreno used his car that week only to travel back and forth to school. On Wednesday evening, Mr. Moreno's odometer read 67,380 miles. How far does Mr. Moreno live from school? How can you model this problem with the base-ten pieces?

Students must first subtract 67,380 miles – 67,236 miles = 144 miles. Over 3 days, Mr. Moreno took 6 trips. Thus, to find the distance he traveled in each trip, divide 144 miles into 6 equal trips.

We use 1 flat, 4 skinnies, and 4 bits to model the 144 miles as shown in Figure 9. Use 6 strips of paper or some other markers to remind the class of each trip. Divide the miles, represented by the base-ten pieces, into 6 groups. Ask students about how many miles they think each trip was. Ask them to look at the base-ten pieces as they form their estimates. Focus students' estimates by asking whether each pile (or trip) can get a flat (100) each. (No) This means each trip will be less than 100 miles. Break up the flat into 10 skinnies. Then, we have 14 skinnies. Ask:

- *How many skinnies can be given to each pile (trip)?* (2)

The trip will then be twenty-some miles. There are 2 skinnies left over to break into bits, so there are 24 bits. Distribute the bits so each pile (trip) gets 4 bits. Thus, each pile has a total of 24 and we know that Mr. Moreno lives 24 miles from school.

Make sure each group models 144 ÷ 6 with their base-ten pieces. Remind students that we can write the division problem as 144 ÷ 6 or 6 ⟌ 144 . Focus their attention on the related number sentences. Since 144 ÷ 6 = 24, we can say 24 × 6 = 144 or 6 × 24 = 144. Explain to students that multiplying back is a good way to check division. Have students use their calculators or paper-and-pencil multiplication methods to verify these relationships for themselves. Remind them that the number 144 is the **dividend** in this problem, 6 is the **divisor,** and the **quotient** is 24.

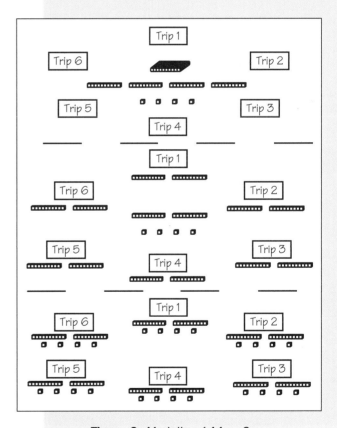

Figure 9: *Modeling 144 ÷ 6*

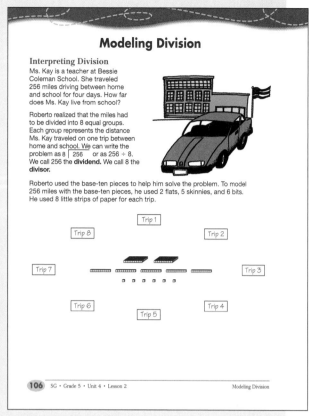

Student Guide - page 106

Ask students to solve several more division problems in their groups using base-ten pieces. For each problem, make sure they estimate the solution first. For example, ask them to solve the following problems:

$$321 \div 3 \qquad 672 \div 7 \qquad 2350 \div 5 \qquad 1048 \div 4$$

For each problem, students should write the appropriate number sentences.

The opening vignette on the *Modeling Division* Activity Pages in the *Student Guide* discusses a problem involving mileage so students have a familiar context when working individually.

Have students complete *Questions 1–9.* If they do not have enough base-ten pieces for all the problems, ask groups to share, use paper models, or base-ten shorthand. Make sure students have calculators available.

Questions 10–11 in the *Student Guide* ask students to mentally compute quotients. To help students do problems that involve zeros in both dividend and divisor, look at the following problems:

$$8 \div 2$$
$$80 \div 2$$
$$80 \div 20$$
$$800 \div 20$$
$$8000 \div 200$$
$$\text{etc.}$$

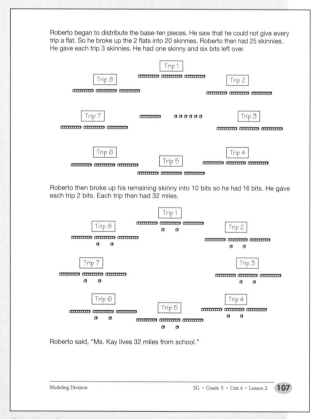

Student Guide - page 107

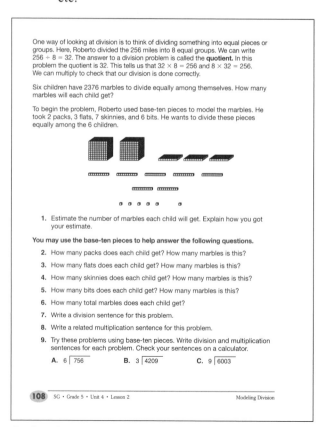

Student Guide - page 108 *(Answers on p. 64)*

To compute 80 ÷ 20, discuss first what the problem is asking: by what number do you multiply 20 to get 80 or how many 20s are there in 80. Children can also use their calculators to find the quotient. Continue with dividing 20 into 800; 8000; 80,000; etc., and ask students if they see a pattern.

Most likely they will see a relationship between the number of zeros in the dividend, divisor, and quotient. Continue with several more examples. Ask students if they can predict the number of zeros that will appear in a quotient. One way to determine the number of zeros is to cancel out zeros in the divisor and the dividend. We are dividing both divisor and dividend by powers of ten. For example, in the problem 80,000 ÷ 200 there are 4 zeros in the dividend and 2 zeros in the divisor. Thus, all but two of the zeros cancel out. Then, 800 ÷ 2 is 400. Warn students about problems such as 400 ÷ 50. No zeros remain because 40 ÷ 5 = 8. Students should be familiar with these patterns as they have explored similar relationships with the fact families.

Homework **Questions 1–7** can be assigned after Part 1.

Part 2 **Interpreting Remainders**
Pose the following problem:

Mr. Moreno found 596 pieces of construction paper. The students are divided into 8 groups to work on an art project. If Mr. Moreno wants to divide the pages evenly, how many pieces does each group get?

Have students estimate first, and then model the problem using base-ten pieces or base-ten shorthand. Students will find that each group gets 74 pieces of construction paper but there are 4 pieces left over. This is the **remainder.**

Have students compute the problem on their calculators and describe what they see. The calculator will show 74.5 as shown in Figure 10.

Ask students to explain this and think about the number sentences they can write for this problem.

Responses will vary. Students may suggest that each group of students gets 74 pages of paper. Then, since there are 4 pages of paper left over, each group could get half a page of paper. Students may interpret the .5 on the calculator display correctly as half a page of paper.

Through whole class discussion, students should also see that:

74 × 8 = 592. By adding the remainder 4, we get 74 × 8 + 4 = 596. Similarly, we can write 8 × 74 + 4 = 596.

Roberto remarked that some division problems are easy to do mentally, just like multiplication problems.

Try these division problems. Check them on a calculator.

10.	A.	6 ÷ 2	B.	9 ÷ 3	C.	12 ÷ 3	D.	40 ÷ 5
		60 ÷ 2		90 ÷ 3		120 ÷ 3		400 ÷ 5
		600 ÷ 2		900 ÷ 3		1200 ÷ 3		4000 ÷ 5
		6000 ÷ 2		9000 ÷ 3		12,000 ÷ 3		40,000 ÷ 5
		60,000 ÷ 2		90,000 ÷ 3		120,000 ÷ 3		400,000 ÷ 5
11.	A.	60 ÷ 30	B.	90 ÷ 10	C.	240 ÷ 60	D.	450 ÷ 50
		600 ÷ 30		900 ÷ 10		2400 ÷ 60		4500 ÷ 50
		600 ÷ 300		900 ÷ 100		2400 ÷ 600		4500 ÷ 500
		6000 ÷ 30		9000 ÷ 10		24,000 ÷ 60		45,000 ÷ 50
		6000 ÷ 300		9000 ÷ 100		24,000 ÷ 600		45,000 ÷ 500

Interpreting Remainders
Before school began at Wentworth Elementary School, there were 165 students enrolled in the fifth grade. If there are six fifth-grade classrooms, how many students are in each class? (There are about the same number of students in each class.)

Roberto modeled this problem with the base-ten shorthand. He used 1 flat, 6 skinnies, and 5 bits to represent the students. He needed to break up these pieces into 6 equal groups.

12. About how many students do you think are in each class? Explain your reasoning.

Modeling Division   SG • Grade 5 • Unit 4 • Lesson 2   **109**

Student Guide - page 109 (Answers on p. 64)

Content Note

Remainders. While it is correct to say that the remainder is 0 for a problem such as 24 divided by 3, it is fine to say, "There is no remainder," since there is nothing left to distribute.

Figure 10: *596 ÷ 8 on the calculator*

TIMS Tip

We will review order of operations more thoroughly in Lesson 5. For now, illustrate on the calculator that computing 5 × 164 first and then adding 1 gives the correct answer to 5 × 164 + 1 = 821. If the addition is done first, the answer may not be correct.

Roberto divided the base-ten pieces evenly. He found there are 2 skinnies and 7 bits in each group with 3 bits left over. The bits left over are called the **remainder**.

Class 1
Class 6   Class 2

. . .

Class 5
Class 4   Class 3

13. How many students are in each class?

14. What do the remaining 3 bits mean?

15. How will the 165 students be divided among the 6 classes?

We say 165 ÷ 6 is 27 with remainder 3. We can write 27 R3. 165 = 6 × 27 + 3.

A school district bought 670 computers to be shared by 7 schools. Roberto computed 670 ÷ 7 on his calculator to find the number of computers each school received. His calculator window showed:

| 95.714286 |

16. What does the 95 mean?

17. What do the numbers to the right of the decimal point tell you?

18. Multiply 95 × 7. This is the number of computers distributed if each school gets 95 computers.

19. How many computers are left to be distributed?

20. Fill in the missing number: 95 × 7 + ? = 670.

110   SG • Grade 5 • Unit 4 • Lesson 2   Modeling Division

Student Guide - page 110 *(Answers on p. 65)*

Ask students to do several more examples, stressing the remainders and the number sentences that go with the problems. Have students also compute the problems on their calculators. They may have difficulty interpreting some of the decimals. Have them look at the whole number part of the display. To find the remainder, multiply the whole number part of the display by the divisor. Then, subtract this number from the dividend. For example,

$821 \div 5$ computed on a calculator yields 164.2. Since $164 \times 5 = 820$, the remainder is $821 - 820 = 1$. Since we can write $821 \div 5 = 164$ remainder 1, then $5 \times 164 + 1 = 821$.

More examples to do in class:

$$633 \div 2 \quad 1023 \div 7 \quad 594 \div 9$$

Students should complete *Questions 12–20* in the *Student Guide*. The division problems contain remainders, and students interpret quotients from calculator calculations. They should check their work by writing number sentences.

In *Questions 16–20* students look at $670 \div 7$ which yields 95.714286 on the calculator. Students should realize that each school will receive 95 computers *(Question 16)*. The decimals tell us that there is a remainder *(Question 17)*. Since $95 \times 7 = 665$ and $670 - 665 = 5$, the remainder is 5 so there are 5 computers left to distribute *(Question 19)*.

Content Note

Calculators and Remainders. The number of digits displayed varies from calculator to calculator. The examples given here show a calculator display with 8 digits.

Many calculators can provide quotients with whole-number remainders rather than decimals. This is sometimes refererred to as "integer division." Even if your calculators have this capability, briefly comparing the two types of answers is worthwhile at this point as it will help students interpret the meaning of the decimal remainders. This concept will be explored in greater detail in Unit 9, after students gain greater familiarity with decimals and fractions.

You can assign Homework *Questions 8–15* in the *Student Guide* after Part 2.

Math Facts

DPP item E provides practice for the multiplication facts for the square numbers.

Homework and Practice

- Homework problems are in the *Student Guide*.
- Assign DPP Tasks F and H. Task F discusses square units. Task H reviews fractions.
- DPP item G provides practice with paper-and-pencil multiplication.

Assessment

- Ask student groups to model problems for you. Ask them what the remainders (if any) mean. You may wish to use the *Observational Assessment Record* to record your observations.
- A quiz on paper-and-pencil division is at the end of Lesson 3.

For Questions 1–4:
- Use base-ten shorthand to sketch the problem and find the solution.
- Write a division sentence for the problem.
- Write a multiplication sentence for the problem.

1. $144 \div 3$
2. $364 \div 7$
3. $603 \div 3$
4. $1856 \div 8$

Compute the following quotients.

5. **A.** $6 \div 2$ **B.** $14 \div 7$ **C.** $27 \div 9$ **D.** $48 \div 6$
   $60 \div 2$ $140 \div 7$ $270 \div 9$ $480 \div 6$
   $600 \div 2$ $1400 \div 7$ $2700 \div 9$ $4800 \div 6$
   $6000 \div 2$ $14,000 \div 7$ $27,000 \div 9$ $48,000 \div 6$

6. **A.** $5 \div 5$ **B.** $28 \div 7$ **C.** $42 \div 6$ **D.** $25 \div 5$
   $50 \div 50$ $280 \div 70$ $420 \div 60$ $250 \div 50$
   $500 \div 50$ $2800 \div 70$ $4200 \div 60$ $2500 \div 50$
   $5000 \div 50$ $28,000 \div 70$ $42,000 \div 60$ $25,000 \div 50$
   $50,000 \div 50$ $280,000 \div 700$ $420,000 \div 6000$ $250,000 \div 5000$

7. Fill in the missing numbers:
   A. Since $57 \times 8 = 456$, then $456 \div 8 = ?$
   B. Since $9 \times 412 = 3708$, then $3708 \div 9 = ?$
   C. Since $1014 \times ? = 6084$, then $6084 \div 6 = 1014$

Use base-ten shorthand to find the solutions to Questions 8 and 9. Estimate first to see if your answer is reasonable. Explain any remainders.

8. A high school has 5 computer labs. The school bought 148 computers. If each computer lab is to get about the same number of computers, how many new computers will each lab get?

9. A CD rack holds 276 CDs. There are 6 sections, which all hold the same number of CDs. How many CDs does each section hold?

Modeling Division   SG • Grade 5 • Unit 4 • Lesson 2   **111**

Student Guide - page 111 *(Answers on pp. 65–66)*

10. Blanca computed $473 \div 4$ on her calculator. The calculator display showed:

    118.25

    A. What does the 118 mean?
    B. What does the .25 mean?
    C. Fill in the number that makes the statement true: $118 \times 4 + ? = 473$.
    D. What is the remainder?

    $$\begin{array}{r} 118 \text{ R }? \\ 4\overline{)473} \end{array}$$

11. Fill in the missing numbers.
    A. $360 \div 9 = n$ **B.** $120 \div n = 40$ **C.** $360 \div n = 90$
    D. $n \div 5 = 30$ **E.** $n \div 6 = 30$ **F.** $4900 \div n = 70$
    G. $400 \div n = 5$ **H.** $160 \div n = 4$ **I.** $3276 \div 4 = n$

Estimate the answers to Questions 12–15.

12. A fifth-grade math textbook has 427 pages. If the 8 chapters are all about the same length, about how many pages are in each chapter?

13. A school spent $2400 on graphing calculators. Each calculator costs $80. How many calculators did the school buy?

14. A school can purchase regular calculators for $11.25 each. If they buy 245 calculators, about how much money will they spend?

15. The volleyball club spent $320.72 for t-shirts. They bought 38 t-shirts. About how much did each t-shirt cost?

112   SG • Grade 5 • Unit 4 • Lesson 2   Modeling Division

Student Guide - page 112 *(Answers on p. 67)*

At a Glance

Math Facts and Daily Practice and Problems

Complete items E–H and continue reviewing the multiplication and division facts for the square numbers.

Part 1. Interpreting Division

1. Use the base-ten pieces to model the division problem $144 \div 6$.
2. Write related multiplication and division sentences, such as $144 \div 6 = 24$ so $24 \times 6 = 144$.
3. Review the terms dividend, divisor, and quotient.
4. Model several more division problems with base-ten pieces. Stress estimating quotients.
5. Discuss mentally dividing numbers with ending zeros.
6. Students complete *Questions 1–11* on the *Modeling Division* Activity Pages in the *Student Guide*.

Part 2. Interpreting Remainders

1. Model $564 \div 8$ using base-ten pieces.
2. Discuss the division problems with remainders on the calculator.
3. Discuss related number sentences: Since $596 \div 8 = 74$ remainder 4, then $74 \times 8 + 4 = 596$.
4. Students complete *Questions 12–20* on the *Modeling Division* Activity Pages in the *Student Guide*.

Homework

Assign Homework *Questions 1–15* in the *Student Guide*.

Assessment

Use the *Observational Assessment Record* to record students' abilities to model division with base-ten pieces.

Answer Key is on pages 64–67.

Notes:

Multiplication Table

×	0	1	2	3	4	5	6	7	8	9	10
0	0	0	0	0	0	0	0	0	0	0	0
1	0	1	2	3	4	5	6	7	8	9	10
2	0	2	4	6	8	10	12	14	16	18	20
3	0	3	6	9	12	15	18	21	24	27	30
4	0	4	8	12	16	20	24	28	32	36	40
5	0	5	10	15	20	25	30	35	40	45	50
6	0	6	12	18	24	30	36	42	48	54	60
7	0	7	14	21	28	35	42	49	56	63	70
8	0	8	16	24	32	40	48	56	64	72	80
9	0	9	18	27	36	45	54	63	72	81	90
10	0	10	20	30	40	50	60	70	80	90	100

×	0	1	2	3	4	5	6	7	8	9	10
0	0	0	0	0	0	0	0	0	0	0	0
1	0	1	2	3	4	5	6	7	8	9	10
2	0	2	4	6	8	10	12	14	16	18	20
3	0	3	6	9	12	15	18	21	24	27	30
4	0	4	8	12	16	20	24	28	32	36	40
5	0	5	10	15	20	25	30	35	40	45	50
6	0	6	12	18	24	30	36	42	48	54	60
7	0	7	14	21	28	35	42	49	56	63	70
8	0	8	16	24	32	40	48	56	64	72	80
9	0	9	18	27	36	45	54	63	72	81	90
10	0	10	20	30	40	50	60	70	80	90	100

×	0	1	2	3	4	5	6	7	8	9	10
0	0	0	0	0	0	0	0	0	0	0	0
1	0	1	2	3	4	5	6	7	8	9	10
2	0	2	4	6	8	10	12	14	16	18	20
3	0	3	6	9	12	15	18	21	24	27	30
4	0	4	8	12	16	20	24	28	32	36	40
5	0	5	10	15	20	25	30	35	40	45	50
6	0	6	12	18	24	30	36	42	48	54	60
7	0	7	14	21	28	35	42	49	56	63	70
8	0	8	16	24	32	40	48	56	64	72	80
9	0	9	18	27	36	45	54	63	72	81	90
10	0	10	20	30	40	50	60	70	80	90	100

×	0	1	2	3	4	5	6	7	8	9	10
0	0	0	0	0	0	0	0	0	0	0	0
1	0	1	2	3	4	5	6	7	8	9	10
2	0	2	4	6	8	10	12	14	16	18	20
3	0	3	6	9	12	15	18	21	24	27	30
4	0	4	8	12	16	20	24	28	32	36	40
5	0	5	10	15	20	25	30	35	40	45	50
6	0	6	12	18	24	30	36	42	48	54	60
7	0	7	14	21	28	35	42	49	56	63	70
8	0	8	16	24	32	40	48	56	64	72	80
9	0	9	18	27	36	45	54	63	72	81	90
10	0	10	20	30	40	50	60	70	80	90	100

Base-Ten Pieces Masters

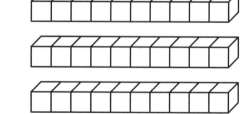

Blackline Master

Name _____ Date _____

Base-Ten Pieces Masters

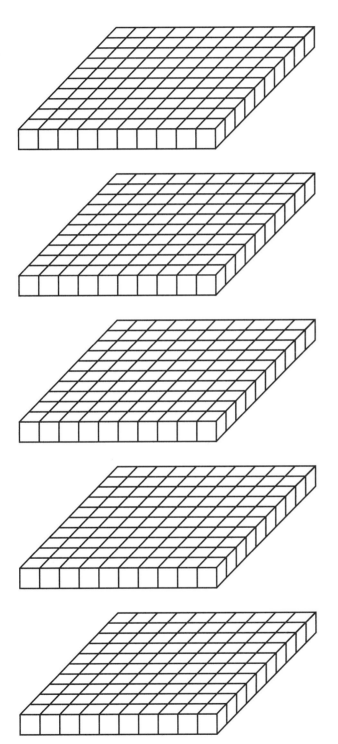

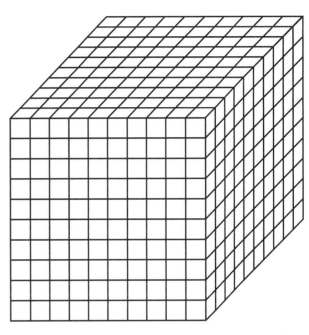

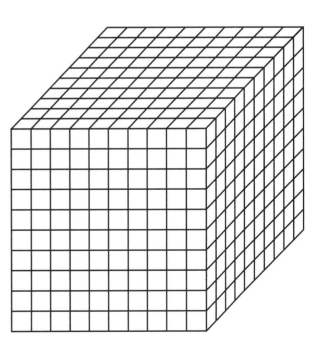

One way of looking at division is to think of dividing something into equal pieces or groups. Here, Roberto divided the 256 miles into 8 equal groups. We can write 256 ÷ 8 = 32. The answer to a division problem is called the **quotient**. In this problem the quotient is 32. This tells us that 32 × 8 = 256 and 8 × 32 = 256. We can multiply to check that our division is done correctly.

Six children have 2376 marbles to divide equally among themselves. How many marbles will each child get?

To begin the problem, Roberto used base-ten pieces to model the marbles. He took 2 packs, 3 flats, 7 skinnies, and 6 bits. He wants to divide these pieces equally among the 6 children.

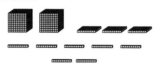

1. Estimate the number of marbles each child will get. Explain how you got your estimate.

You may use the base-ten pieces to help answer the following questions.

2. How many packs does each child get? How many marbles is this?
3. How many flats does each child get? How many marbles is this?
4. How many skinnies does each child get? How many marbles is this?
5. How many bits does each child get? How many marbles is this?
6. How many total marbles does each child get?
7. Write a division sentence for this problem.
8. Write a related multiplication sentence for this problem.
9. Try these problems using base-ten pieces. Write division and multiplication sentences for each problem. Check your sentences on a calculator.
   A. 6⟌756   B. 3⟌4209   C. 9⟌6003

Student Guide - page 108

Roberto remarked that some division problems are easy to do mentally, just like multiplication problems.

Try these division problems. Check them on a calculator.

10. A. 6 ÷ 2   B. 9 ÷ 3   C. 12 ÷ 3   D. 40 ÷ 5
       60 ÷ 2   90 ÷ 3   120 ÷ 3   400 ÷ 5
       600 ÷ 2   900 ÷ 3   1200 ÷ 3   4000 ÷ 5
       6000 ÷ 2   9000 ÷ 3   12,000 ÷ 3   40,000 ÷ 5
       60,000 ÷ 2   90,000 ÷ 3   120,000 ÷ 3   400,000 ÷ 5

11. A. 60 ÷ 30   B. 90 ÷ 10   C. 240 ÷ 60   D. 450 ÷ 50
       600 ÷ 30   900 ÷ 10   2400 ÷ 60   4500 ÷ 50
       600 ÷ 300   900 ÷ 100   2400 ÷ 600   4500 ÷ 500
       6000 ÷ 30   9000 ÷ 10   24,000 ÷ 60   45,000 ÷ 50
       6000 ÷ 300   9000 ÷ 100   24,000 ÷ 600   45,000 ÷ 500

Interpreting Remainders
Before school began at Wentworth Elementary School, there were 165 students enrolled in the fifth grade. If there are six fifth-grade classrooms, how many students are in each class? (There are about the same number of students in each class.)

Roberto modeled this problem with the base-ten shorthand. He used 1 flat, 6 skinnies, and 5 bits to represent the students. He needed to break up these pieces into 6 equal groups.

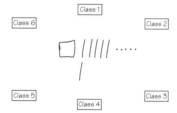

12. About how many students do you think are in each class? Explain your reasoning.

Student Guide - page 109

Student Guide (p. 108)

1. Estimates will vary. One possible estimate is 2400 marbles ÷ 6 children = 400 marbles per child. Since the 2 packs can be exchanged for 20 flats—20 flats ÷ 6 is about 3 flats or 300 marbles per group.
2. 0 packs; 0 marbles
3. 3 flats; 300 marbles
4. 9 skinnies; 90 marbles
5. 6 bits; 6 marbles
6. 396 marbles
7. 2376 ÷ 6 = 396
8. 396 × 6 = 2376
9. A. 756 ÷ 6 = 126; 126 × 6 = 756
   B. 4209 ÷ 3 = 1403; 1403 × 3 = 4209
   C. 6003 ÷ 9 = 667; 667 × 9 = 6003

Student Guide (p. 109)

10. A. 3; 30; 300; 3000; 30,000
    B. 3; 30; 300; 3000; 30,000
    C. 4; 40; 400; 4000; 40,000
    D. 8; 80; 800; 8000; 80,000
11. A. 2; 20; 2; 200; 20
    B. 9; 90; 9; 900; 90
    C. 4; 40; 4; 400; 40
    D. 9; 90; 9; 900; 90
12. Estimates will vary. One possible estimate is about 30; 170 students ÷ 6 classrooms is between 20 (20 × 6 = 120) and 30 students (30 × 6 = 180) per classroom.

Student Guide (p. 110)

13. $165 \div 6 = 27$ R3; 27 students in three classes and 28 students in three classes

14. 3 remaining students

15. 27 students in three classes and 28 students in three classes

16. Each school will receive 95 computers.*

17. There is a remainder.*

18. 665 computers

19. 5 computers*

20. $95 \times 7 + 5 = 670$

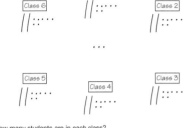

Roberto divided the base-ten pieces evenly. He found there are 2 skinnies and 7 bits in each group with 3 bits left over. The bits left over are called the **remainder**.

Class 1
Class 6   Class 2

· · ·

Class 5   Class 4   Class 3

13. How many students are in each class?

14. What do the remaining 3 bits mean?

15. How will the 165 students be divided among the 6 classes?

We say $165 \div 6$ is 27 with remainder 3. We can write 27 R3. $165 = 6 \times 27 + 3$.

A school district bought 670 computers to be shared by 7 schools. Roberto computed $670 \div 7$ on his calculator to find the number of computers each school received. His calculator window showed:

95.714286

16. What does the 95 mean?

17. What do the numbers to the right of the decimal point tell you?

18. Multiply 95×7. This is the number of computers distributed if each school gets 95 computers.

19. How many computers are left to be distributed?

20. Fill in the missing number: $95 \times 7 + ? = 670$.

Student Guide - page 110

Student Guide (p. 111)

Homework

1. $144 \div 3 = 48; 48 \times 3 = 144$

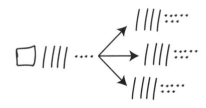

2. $364 \div 7 = 52; 52 \times 7 = 364$

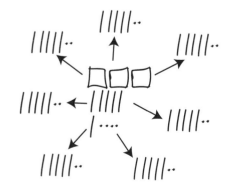

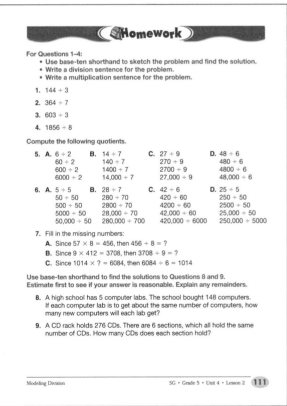

Homework

For Questions 1–4:
• Use base-ten shorthand to sketch the problem and find the solution.
• Write a division sentence for the problem.
• Write a multiplication sentence for the problem.

1. $144 \div 3$

2. $364 \div 7$

3. $603 \div 3$

4. $1856 \div 8$

Compute the following quotients.

5. A. $6 \div 2$ **B.** $14 \div 7$ **C.** $27 \div 9$ **D.** $48 \div 6$
$60 \div 2$ $140 \div 7$ $270 \div 9$ $480 \div 6$
$600 \div 2$ $1400 \div 7$ $2700 \div 9$ $4800 \div 6$
$6000 \div 2$ $14,000 \div 7$ $27,000 \div 9$ $48,000 \div 6$

6. A. $5 \div 5$ **B.** $28 \div 7$ **C.** $42 \div 6$ **D.** $25 \div 5$
$50 \div 50$ $280 \div 70$ $420 \div 60$ $250 \div 50$
$500 \div 50$ $2800 \div 70$ $4200 \div 60$ $2500 \div 50$
$5000 \div 50$ $28,000 \div 700$ $42,000 \div 60$ $25,000 \div 50$
$50,000 \div 50$ $280,000 \div 700$ $420,000 \div 6000$ $250,000 \div 5000$

7. Fill in the missing numbers:
A. Since $57 \times 8 = 456$, then $456 \div 8 = ?$
B. Since $9 \times 412 = 3708$, then $3708 \div 9 = ?$
C. Since $1014 \times ? = 6084$, then $6084 \div 6 = 1014$

Use base-ten shorthand to find the solutions to Questions 8 and 9. Estimate first to see if your answer is reasonable. Explain any remainders.

8. A high school has 5 computer labs. The school bought 148 computers. If each computer lab is to get about the same number of computers, how many new computers will each lab get?

9. A CD rack holds 276 CDs. There are 6 sections, which all hold the same number of CDs. How many CDs does each section hold?

Student Guide - page 111

*Answers and/or discussion are included in the Lesson Guide.

3. $603 \div 3 = 201; 201 \times 3 = 603$

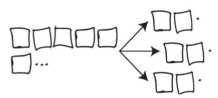

4. $1856 \div 8 = 232; 232 \times 8 = 1856$

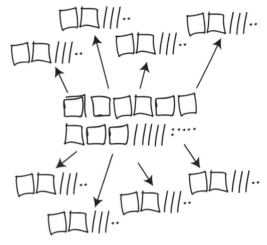

5. A. 3; 30; 300; 3000

   B. 2; 20; 200; 2000

   C. 3; 30; 300; 3000

   D. 8; 80; 800; 8000

6. A. 1; 1; 10; 100; 1000

   B. 4; 4; 40; 400; 400

   C. 7; 7; 70; 700; 70

   D. 5; 5; 50; 500; 50

7. A. 57

   B. 412

   C. 6

8. Estimates will vary. One possible estimate is 150 computers $\div$ 5 labs = 30 computers per lab. The actual solution is shown below. There is a remainder of 3 computers, so three labs will each get one extra computer.

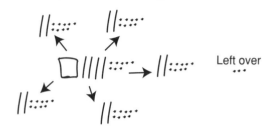

9. Estimates will vary. One possible estimate is 300 CDs $\div$ 6 sections = 50 CDs per section. The actual solution is shown below.

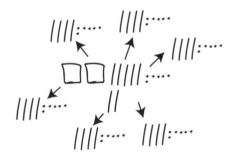

Student Guide (p. 112)

10. A. 4 divides 473: 118 times

B. There is a remainder.

C. $118 \times 4 + 1 = 473$

D. 1

11. A. 40   **B.** 3

C. 4   **D.** 150

E. 180   **F.** 70

G. 80   **H.** 40

I. 814

Estimates will vary for *Questions 12–15.* One possible estimate is shown for each.

12. 400 pages ÷ 8 chapters = 50 pages per chapter

13. $2400.00 ÷ $80.00 per calculator = 30 calculators

14. $10.00 per calculator × 250 calculators = $2500.00

15. $320.00 ÷ 40 t-shirts = $8.00 per t-shirt

---

10. Blanca computed 473 ÷ 4 on her calculator. The calculator display showed:

> 118.25

  A. What does the 118 mean?
  B. What does the .25 mean?
  C. Fill in the number that makes the statement true: 118 × 4 + ? = 473.
  D. What is the remainder?

$$\frac{118\ R\ ?}{4\ \overline{\smash{)}\ 473}}$$

11. Fill in the missing numbers.
  A. 360 ÷ 9 = n   **B.** 120 ÷ n = 40   **C.** 360 ÷ n = 90
  D. n ÷ 5 = 30   **E.** n ÷ 6 = 30   **F.** 4900 ÷ n = 70
  G. 400 ÷ n = 5   **H.** 160 ÷ n = 4   **I.** 3276 ÷ 4 = n

Estimate the answers to Questions 12–15.

12. A fifth-grade math textbook has 427 pages. If the 8 chapters are all about the same length, about how many pages are in each chapter?

13. A school spent $2400 on graphing calculators. Each calculator costs $80. How many calculators did the school buy?

14. A school can purchase regular calculators for $11.25 each. If they buy 245 calculators, about how much money will they spend?

15. The volleyball club spent $320.72 for t-shirts. They bought 38 t-shirts. About how much did each t-shirt cost?

Student Guide - page 112

Lesson 3

Paper-and-Pencil Division

Lesson Overview

A paper-and-pencil method of division, called the forgiving method, is reviewed. Students continue to estimate quotients and interpret remainders.

Key Content

- Dividing using a paper-and-pencil method with 1-digit divisors.
- Interpreting remainders.
- Estimating quotients.

Key Vocabulary

- forgiving division method

Math Facts

Complete DPP items I, K, and M and continue reviewing the multiplication and division facts for the square numbers.

Homework

1. Assign the Homework section in the *Student Guide* over several nights.
2. Assign Part 3 of the Home Practice.

Assessment

Students complete the *Quiz* Assessment Page.

Curriculum Sequence

Before This Unit

Paper-and-pencil division was introduced in Unit 13 of fourth grade.

After This Unit

In Unit 9 students will focus on paper-and-pencil division with two-digit divisors.

Materials List

Supplies and Copies

Student	Teacher
Supplies for Each Student • calculator **Supplies for Each Student Pair** • 1 set of base-ten pieces (2 packs, 14 flats, 30 skinnies, 50 bits)	**Supplies** • overhead base-ten pieces, optional
Copies • 1 copy of *Quiz* per student (*Unit Resource Guide* Page 76)	**Copies/Transparencies**

All blackline masters including assessment, transparency, and DPP masters are also on the Teacher Resource CD.

Student Books

Paper-and-Pencil Division (*Student Guide* Pages 113–117)

Daily Practice and Problems and Home Practice

DPP items I–N (*Unit Resource Guide* Pages 22–24)
Home Practice Part 3 (*Discovery Assignment Book* Page 44)

Note: Classrooms whose pacing differs significantly from the suggested pacing of the units should use the Math Facts Calendar in Section 4 of the *Facts Resource Guide* to ensure students receive the complete math facts program.

Daily Practice and Problems

Suggestions for using the DPPs are on page 74.

I. Bit: Fact Families for the Square Numbers (URG p. 22)

The square numbers only have two facts in each fact family.

For example, the following two facts are in the same fact family.

$$2 \times 2 = 4 \text{ and } 4 \div 2 = 2$$

Solve the fact. Then name the second fact in the same fact family.

A. $9 \times 9 = ?$ B. $5 \times 5 = ?$
C. $7 \times 7 = ?$ D. $8 \times 8 = ?$
E. $10 \times 10 = ?$ F. $3 \times 3 = ?$
G. $6 \times 6 = ?$ H. $4 \times 4 = ?$

J. Task: Time (URG p. 22)

1. Jerome is excited about going to a professional basketball game. He is counting the hours. Today is Monday. The time is 7:00 A.M. In 36 hours the basketball game begins. What day is Jerome attending the game? At what time does the game begin?
2. Shannon fell off her bicycle. She got 10 stitches in her hand. The doctor told her to keep her hand dry for 72 hours. She leaves the doctor's office at 3:30 P.M. on Wednesday. When will the 72 hours be up?

K. Bit: Fact Families for × and ÷ (URG p. 23)

Complete the number sentences for the related facts.

A. $2 \times 2 = $ ___   B. $8 \times 8 = $ ___
   ___ $\div 2 = $ ___   ___ $\div$ ___ $= 8$

C. $36 \div 6 = $ ___   D. $10 \times$ ___ $= 100$
   ___ $\times 6 = $ ___ $100 \div$ ___ $= $ ___

L. Challenge: Which Is Greater? (URG p. 23)

For each pair of numbers, tell which is greater. Show how you know.

A. 3×10^4 or 7×10^2?
B. 2×10^2 or 20,000?
C. 79,300,000 or 7.93×10^5?
D. $40,000,000,000 \times 5$ or 2×10^9?
E. 3.2×10^{11} or thirty-two trillion?

M. Bit: Fact Families for × and ÷ (URG p. 24)

Complete the number sentences for the related facts.

A. $3 \times 3 = $ ___   B. $7 \times 7 = $ ___
   ___ $\div 3 = $ ___   ___ $\div 7 = $ ___

C. $9 \times 9 = $ ___   D. $25 \div 5 = $ ___
   ___ $\div 9 = $ ___   ___ $\times 5 = $ ___

E. $4 \times 4 = $ ___
   ___ $\div$ ___ $= 4$

N. Task: Fractions (URG p. 24)

1. The two squares shown here together represent $\frac{1}{4}$.

A. Draw one whole.
B. Write a fraction for one of the two squares shown above.

2. If the shape below represents $\frac{1}{6}$, show $\frac{1}{2}$.

Teaching the Activity

The greatest difficulty students have with paper-and-pencil division is choosing the correct partial quotient. Often students estimate too high or too low, causing much frustration. The **forgiving division method** helps alleviate this problem. The forgiving method is the paper-and-pencil method we use to divide.

Pose the problem:

A box contains 644 beads. If the beads are shared equally among 7 children, how many beads does each child get?

Remind students that they can use base-ten pieces to solve this problem. Have the base-ten pieces available for students to use when needed.

Ask children to estimate the quotient. Ask them whether they think the number is more than 100. In other words, will each child get more than 100 beads? Most should see that 100 is too high ($7 \times 100 = 700$).

To illustrate the forgiving method, ask students to pick a number. This will be the number of beads each child gets in the first round of distributing the beads. Children without previous estimation experience in division often take wild guesses. This is fine, as long as it is not more than 92, any number will work. The only time we need to erase in the forgiving method is if we choose too high. Suggest to students to use easy numbers (numbers ending in zeros are nice) at the beginning. Figure 11 shows an example with 20 as a first guess, then 50, 20 again, and finally 2.

```
           92
      ┌────────
    7 │ 644
      │ -140      20
      │ ─────
      │  504
      │ -350      50
      │ ─────
      │  154
      │ -140      20
      │ ─────
      │   14
      │  -14       2
      │ ─────    ────
      │    0      92
```

Figure 11: *Forgiving algorithm*

Choosing 20 as a first number means we give 20 beads to each child, so 140 beads are distributed and 504 beads remain. Then estimate the number of times 7 goes into 504. In this example we estimate 50 times. Then multiply 50 times 7 to get 350 and subtract. There are 154 beads left to be distributed. Continue in this manner until there are no more beads

TIMS Tip

Perhaps some students in your class have learned the traditional long division method or another method. Plan time for these students to show their methods as well. While we have chosen the forgiving method, students should realize that there are many division methods.

Paper-and-Pencil Division

The Good-For-You Bakery baked 425 banana walnut muffins. They packaged them in packages of 6. How many packages of banana walnut muffins did they make?

Nila says she knows a paper-and-pencil method for doing division. She calls this the **forgiving division method.** Nila thought about the base-ten pieces as she did the problem. The base-ten pieces can represent the muffins.

Nila wrote the problem like this:

$$6\,\overline{|\,425}$$

"To use the forgiving method, I make an estimate about the number of packages I think they made. My first estimate is 20."

```
6 | 425
  -120   20
   305
```

"Since 20 × 6 = 120, this means I have taken care of 120 muffins. There are 305 still to be packaged. This time I'll choose a larger number: 40. Since 40 × 6 = 240, this means I have packaged 240 more muffins. There are 65 muffins left to package."

```
6 | 425
  -120   20
   305
  -240   40
    65
```

Student Guide - page 113

"Now I know 10 × 6 = 60, so I can make 10 more packages with 5 muffins remaining."

```
        70 R5
6 | 425
  -120    20
   305
  -240    40
    65
   -60    10
     5    70
```

"So, altogether, 70 packages of muffins can be made with 5 muffins left."

We can write:

$$6 \times 70 + 5 = 425$$

A box of marbles contains 5386 marbles. The marbles are to be shared equally among 8 children. How many marbles does each child get?

Nila wrote the problem like this:

$$8\,\overline{|\,5386}$$

"To use the forgiving method, I make an estimate about the number of marbles each child will get. My first guess is 300. That's like giving 3 flats to each child, so I write:

```
8 | 5386
  -2400   300
   2986
```

"Since 8 × 300 = 2400, this means I have taken care of 2400 of the marbles. I still have 2986 left to distribute. The 300 means each child has already gotten 300 marbles. Now I guess at how many more marbles I can give each child. I'll use 300 again, since 2400 will take care of a lot of the 2986 remaining. Now I have 586 left."

```
8 | 5386
  -2400   300
   2986
  -2400   300
    586
```

Student Guide - page 114

---

to distribute. Since we distributed 20, then 50, 20, and 2 beads, each child receives $20 + 50 + 20 + 2 = 92$ beads. After finishing the problem, write the quotient (92) above the dividend as usual.

Since: $644 \div 7 = 92$ we can write $92 \times 7 = 644$ or $7 \times 92 = 644$.

Practice the forgiving division method with several more problems.

$$448 \div 8 \qquad 985 \div 5 \qquad 3456 \div 9 \qquad 759 \div 4$$

For each problem, ask students to estimate their answer first. Remind them that thinking about the base-ten pieces is often helpful. For example, to estimate $759 \div 4$ we can think about distributing 7 flats between 4 piles. We immediately know the answer will be more than 100 since each pile gets a flat. Since we have 2 more flats to divide, we can estimate that the answer will be more than 150, but less than 200.

Ask students to also compute the problems on a calculator and write number sentences. This emphasizes the relationship between multiplication and division as well as how to interpret division on a calculator.

As another example with a remainder,

A large grocery store baked 2349 cookies. They packaged the cookies in packages of 8. How many packages of cookies did they make?

Begin by asking students to estimate the number of packages. Will it be over 100? over 1000? Model solving the problem using the forgiving method. Allow students to choose the partial quotients. An example solution is shown in Figure 12.

```
            293 R5
8 | 2349
   - 400      50
    1949
   - 800     100
    1149
   - 800     100
     349
   - 320      40
      29
    - 24       3
       5     293
```

Figure 12: *Computing $2349 \div 8$ using the forgiving method*

Note that in this problem we have a remainder. There are 5 cookies that cannot be packaged. The number of packages they made is 293.

Review writing number sentences:

Since 2349 ÷ 8 = 293 with remainder 5, then
293 × 8 + 5 = 2349 and 8 × 293 + 5 = 2349.

The *Paper-and-Pencil Division* Activity Pages in the *Student Guide* provide practice in understanding the forgiving method. Two examples are discussed. Read through these examples as a class. The first example asks children to find the number of packages of muffins given that 425 muffins were baked and there are 6 muffins in a package. This is an example of partitive division, discussed in the Background. Although it is more difficult to model this situation with base-ten pieces, students can use the base-ten pieces to model dividing 425 into 6 equal groups. Have students complete *Questions A–D* in groups. Ask them to explain the remainders. Assess their understanding by checking each group's progress. Record your observations on the *Observational Assessment Record*. *Questions E–L* provide additional opportunities for practice. Encourage students to make good estimates as they solve the problems.

"I can't use 300 again because it is way too big. I'll try 20. Since 20 × 8 = 160, I have 426 left. I'll try something bigger next."

```
8 ) 5386
   -2400    300
    2986
   -2400    300
     586
    -160    20
     426
```

"I'll try 50. 8 × 50 = 400. Now I have 26 left."

```
8 ) 5386
   -2400    300
    2986
   -2400    300
     586
    -160    20
     426
    -400    50
      26
```

"Now I'll try 3. Since 8 × 3 = 24, there are 2 marbles left over. Then 5386 divided by 8 is 673 (300 + 300 + 20 + 50 + 3) with remainder 2. Each child gets 673 marbles, with 2 left over."

```
      673 R2
8 ) 5386
   -2400    300
    2986
   -2400    300
     586
    -160    20
     426
    -400    50
      26
     -24     3
       2    673
```

Student Guide - page 115

Nila thought about a multiplication sentence for this problem. On her calculator, she found 673 × 8 = 5384. When she added the remainder 2, she got 5386. Another way to write this is to say 673 × 8 + 2 = 5386.

Try these problems, using the forgiving method. Write number sentences for each problem.

A. 4) 856	**B.** 7) 1256	**C.** 547 ÷ 9	**D.** 3476 ÷ 4
E. 8) 901	**F.** 9017 ÷ 8	**G.** 562 ÷ 5	**H.** 5667 ÷ 3
I. 5274 ÷ 2	**J.** 2) 527	**K.** 7) 8413	**L.** 792 ÷ 7

Homework

1. Twenty-four cookies fit on a pan at the Good-For-You Bakery. If the baker makes 16 pans of cookies, how many cookies does he bake?
2. The Good-For-You Bakery has 6 ovens. They bake 173 pies every day and bake about the same number of pies in each oven. About how many pies are baked in each oven?
3. The bakery makes 4 different kinds of breads: whole wheat, rye, oatmeal, and cinnamon. They bake a total of 509 loaves of bread a day. If they bake about the same number of each type, about how many loaves of each bread do they bake?

Compute the following. Use the forgiving method or another method. Do not use a calculator. Remember to check whether your answer seems reasonable.

4. 4) 586	**5.** 3) 904	**6.** 819 ÷ 7
7. 1028 ÷ 6	**8.** 9) 2349	**9.** 2049 ÷ 5

10. Choose one of Questions 4–9. Write a story about it.
11. For a fund-raiser, the members of the Wilderness Club baked 789 chocolate chip cookies.
    A. If they sell them in packages of 5, how many packages can they make?
    B. The Wilderness Club sold 102 packages. How many cookies were left?
12. The club earned $157. They decided to split this money equally into different funds: a party, new equipment, and camping fees. How much money went into each fund?

Student Guide - page 116 (Answers on p. 77)

The following problems are about lawns and plants:

13. There are about 1700 grass plants in 2 square feet of a healthy lawn. About how many plants are in 1 square foot?

14. There are 8 single-family homes on Elm Street in Mathville. The families who live there spend a total of about $1040 a year on grass care. If they spend about the same amount, about how much does each family spend?

15. In 1993, the same families on Elm Street spent a total of about $536 on flower gardens. If they spent about the same amount, about how much did each family spend?

16. Believe it or not, 5 grass plants will produce about 1875 miles of roots in their lifetimes. About how many miles of roots will one plant produce?

17. A store sells tulip bulbs. The bulbs come in packages of 8. If they sold 216 bulbs, about how many packages did they sell?

18. 4122 ÷ 8   19. 4)2601   20. 6)2072

Paper-and-Pencil Division   SG • Grade 5 • Unit 4 • Lesson 3   117

Student Guide - page 117 *(Answers on p. 78)*

Name _____ Date _____

PART 3 Multiplication and Division Practice
Solve the following problems using a paper-and-pencil method. Estimate to be sure your answers are reasonable.

A. 49 × 9 =   B. 135 ÷ 6 =   C. 18 × 45 =   D. 1064 ÷ 4 =

E. 22 × 76 =   F. 2834 ÷ 3 =   G. 8505 ÷ 7 =   H. 1063 × 3 =

I. 1894 × 4 =   J. 7720 ÷ 8 =   K. 2460 × 6 =   L. 8070 ÷ 5 =

44 DAB • Grade 5 • Unit 4   DIVISION AND DATA

Discovery Assignment Book - page 44 *(Answers on p. 78)*

DPP items I, K, and M introduce fact families for the square numbers.

- Homework problems are on the *Paper-and-Pencil Division* Activity Pages in the *Student Guide.* Assign these problems over several nights.

- Assign DPP Task J, which provides practice with time. Task N reviews fraction concepts.

- Assign Part 3 of the Home Practice, which provides multiplication and division practice.

Answers for Part 3 of the Home Practice are in the Answer Key at the end of this lesson and at the end of this unit.

Use the *Quiz* Assessment Page to assess students' understanding of division. Allow students to use base-ten pieces during the quiz.

Assign DPP Challenge L, which reviews number sense involving big numbers and scientific notation.

At a Glance

Math Facts and Daily Practice and Problems

Complete DPP items I–N and continue reviewing the multiplication and division facts for the square numbers.

Teaching the Activity

1. Explain to students the forgiving division method in the context of distributing 644 beads to 7 children.
2. Do several problems using the forgiving method, stressing estimation and relating each problem to the base-ten pieces.
3. Discuss problems involving remainders and related number sentences.
4. Students complete the *Paper-and-Pencil Division* Activity Pages in the *Student Guide.*

Homework

1. Assign the Homework section in the *Student Guide* over several nights.
2. Assign Part 3 of the Home Practice.

Assessment

Students complete the *Quiz* Assessment Page.

Extension

Assign DPP Challenge L.

Answer Key is on pages 77–79.

Notes:

Quiz

**Answer the questions using any method you wish. Show your work.
Calculators are not allowed.**

1. A video store has 8106 videotapes in 6 sections. If each section contains the same number of videotapes, how many videotapes are in each section?

2. The eighth-grade class at Sunny Valley Middle School is going on a field trip. Each bus holds 53 students. If there are 286 eighth graders, will 5 buses be enough? Explain your answer.

Assessment Blackline Master

Student Guide (p. 116)

A. $856 \div 4 = 214$

B. $1256 \div 7 = 179 \text{ R}3$

C. $547 \div 9 = 60 \text{ R}7$

D. $3476 \div 4 = 869$

E. $901 \div 8 = 112 \text{ R}5$

F. $9017 \div 8 = 1127 \text{ R}1$

G. $562 \div 5 = 112 \text{ R}2$

H. $5667 \div 5 = 1133 \text{ R}2$

I. $5274 \div 2 = 2637$

J. $527 \div 2 = 263 \text{ R}1$

K. $8413 \div 7 = 1201 \text{ R}6$

L. $792 \div 7 = 113 \text{ R}1$

Homework

1. 384 cookies

2. 28 pies in one oven and 29 pies in 5 ovens

3. 127 of each type with one type having 128 loaves instead. A good estimate would be 500 loaves ÷ 4 kinds = 125 loaves of each kind

4. 146 R2

5. 301 R1

6. 117

7. 171 R2

8. 261

9. 409 R4

10. Stories will vary. One possible story for *Question 4* follows: There are 586 girls in the school. Each girl belongs to one of four clubs. There are about the same number of girls in each club. About how many girls are in each club?

11. **A.** 157 packages with 4 cookies left over

   B. 55 packages, which have 55 × 5 or 275 cookies in all; adding on the 4 left over cookies—279 cookies.

12. $52.33 and 1 penny left over or $52.33 in each of two funds and $52.34 in the third fund.

Student Guide - page 116

The following problems are about lawns and plants:

13. There are about 1700 grass plants in 2 square feet of a healthy lawn. About how many plants are in 1 square foot?

14. There are 8 single-family homes on Elm Street in Mathville. The families who live there spend a total of about $1040 a year on grass care. If they spend about the same amount, about how much does each family spend?

15. In 1993, the same families on Elm Street spent a total of about $536 on flower gardens. If they spent about the same amount, about how much did each family spend?

16. Believe it or not, 5 grass plants will produce about 1875 miles of roots in their lifetimes. About how many miles of roots will one plant produce?

17. A store sells tulip bulbs. The bulbs come in packages of 8. If they sold 216 bulbs, about how many packages did they sell?

18. 4122 ÷ 8   19. 4⟌2601   20. 6⟌2072

Paper-and-Pencil Division   SG • Grade 5 • Unit 4 • Lesson 3   **117**

Student Guide - page 117

Student Guide (p. 117)

13. Estimates will vary. About 800 grass plants; 850 grass plants.

14. Estimates will vary. Between $100 and $200; about $150.00.

15. Estimates will vary. Between $60 and $70; $65.00

16. Estimates will vary. Between 300 and 400; about 350 miles.

17. About 30 packages

18. $4122 \div 8 = 515 \text{ R}2$

19. $2061 \div 4 = 515 \text{ R}1$

20. $2072 \div 6 = 345 \text{ R}2$

Name _____   Date _____

PART 3 Multiplication and Division Practice

Solve the following problems using a paper-and-pencil method. Estimate to be sure your answers are reasonable.

A. 49 × 9 =   B. 135 ÷ 6 =   C. 18 × 45 =   D. 1064 ÷ 4 =

E. 22 × 76 =   F. 2834 ÷ 3 =   G. 8505 ÷ 7 =   H. 1063 × 3 =

I. 1894 × 4 =   J. 7720 ÷ 8 =   K. 2460 × 6 =   L. 8070 ÷ 5 =

44   DAB • Grade 5 • Unit 4   DIVISION AND DATA

Discovery Assignment Book - page 44

Discovery Assignment Book (p. 44)

Home Practice*

Part 3. Multiplication and Division Practice

A. 441

B. 22 R3

C. 810

D. 266

E. 1672

F. 944 R2

G. 1215

H. 3189

I. 7576

J. 965

K. 14,760

L. 1614

*Answers for all the Home Practice in the *Discovery Assignment Book* are at the end of the unit.

Unit Resource Guide (p. 76)

Quiz

1. 8106 tapes ÷ 6 sections = 1351 tapes per section

2. No, 286 ÷ 5 = 57 R1. Each bus can only hold 53 students; 6 buses will be needed.

Name _____ Date _____

Quiz

Answer the questions using any method you wish. Show your work. Calculators are not allowed.

1. A video store has 8106 videotapes in 6 sections. If each section contains the same number of videotapes, how many videotapes are in each section?

2. The eighth-grade class at Sunny Valley Middle School is going on a field trip. Each bus holds 53 students. If there are 286 eighth graders, will 5 buses be enough? Explain your answer.

76   URG • Grade 5 • Unit 4 • Lesson 3   Assessment Blackline Master

Copyright © Kendall/Hunt Publishing Company

Unit Resource Guide - page 76

Optional Lesson 4

How Close Is Close Enough?

Estimated Class Sessions

2-3

Lesson Overview

This optional lesson has two parts. In Part 1 students estimate the area of irregular shapes by counting square centimeters. The class decides which estimates are "close enough" by finding the median estimate and deciding the estimates that are within 10% of the median. The notion of "closeness" is related to the magnitude of the area. Students learn methods for approximating 10% of a number mentally and with a calculator. They also discuss the idea that whether an estimate for the area of an irregular shape is close or not depends on the size of the area. Students apply these skills in Part 2 of the lesson, which focuses on the *Student Guide* pages.

Key Content

- Averaging: finding the median.
- Estimating the area of shapes with curved sides.
- Estimating 10% of a number.
- Using 10% as a standard for error analysis.

Key Vocabulary

- ten percent (10%)

Homework

Assign the Homework section in the *Student Guide*.

Curriculum Sequence

Before This Unit

Percents

Students were introduced to percents in Grade 3 Unit 14 Lesson 3 *Tracking Our Reading.* They used 25%, 50%, 75%, and 100% as goals in a reading survey. In Grade 4 Unit 6 Lesson 6 *Close Enough,* students were introduced to 10% as a standard for error analysis.

After This Unit

Percents

For the remainder of the year, students can use 10% as a standard for error analysis in some investigations. See the *Spreading Out* lab in this unit for an example. Students study percents in Unit 7. They use percents to report data in the labs in Units 7 and 8.

Materials List

Supplies and Copies

Student	Teacher
Supplies for Each Student • calculator	**Supplies**
Copies • 1 copy of *Shapes 1–5* per student (*Unit Resource Guide* Page 91) • 1 copy of *Shapes 6 and 7* per student (*Unit Resource Guide* Page 92) • 1 copy of *Two-column Data Table* per student group (*Unit Resource Guide* Page 93)	**Copies/Transparencies** • 1 transparency of *Shapes 1–5* (*Unit Resource Guide* Page 91) • 1 transparency of *10% Chart* or large graph paper for a class data table (*Discovery Assignment Book* Page 65) • 1 transparency of *Centimeter Grid Paper,* optional (*Unit Resource Guide* Page 44) • 1 transparency of *Two-column Data Table,* optional (*Unit Resource Guide* Page 93)

All blackline masters including assessment, transparency, and DPP masters are also on the Teacher Resource CD.

Student Books

How Close Is Close Enough? (*Student Guide* Pages 118–122)
10% Chart (*Discovery Assignment Book* Page 65)

In Part 1 of this activity, students work in groups of three or four. Students in each group estimate the area of an irregular shape and compare their estimates. There are seven shapes altogether on the *Shapes 1–5* and *Shapes 6 and 7* Activity Pages in the *Unit Resource Guide.* Assign one shape to each group. Each student only needs one copy of one of these two pages depending on the shape assigned to the group.

Part 1 **Estimating the Area of an Irregular Shape**

To begin the activity, discuss students' strategies for finding the area of a shape with curved sides. Remind them of the irregular shapes they measured in Lesson 1 on the *Strategies to Find Area* Activity Pages in the *Discovery Assignment Book.* Refer to Figures G and H on those pages or sketch an irregular shape on a transparency of *Centimeter Grid Paper.* Review strategies which include:

- enclosing the irregular shape in a rectangle and finding the area of this rectangle for a very rough estimate;

- counting full square centimeters and combining fractional units to make more whole units;

- enclosing the shape in a rectangle, finding the area of the rectangle, and then subtracting the estimated number of square centimeters within the rectangle that are not part of the shape;

- counting all squares completely enclosed by the shape and then counting all squares completely enclosing the shape. Then, average these two areas. See Figure 13 for an example.

After this discussion, ask each group to use one of these methods to estimate the area of one shape on the *Shapes 1–5* or *Shapes 6 and 7* Activity Pages. Each student in the group should estimate the area of the shape. The group members share their measurements by recording them in a data table. Once all members have recorded an estimate, the group finds the median estimated area for their shape. Instruct them to record this information at the top of their data table. Student groups can hand draw the data tables, or you may distribute a *Two-column Data Table* to each group. Two sample data tables are shown in Figure 14.

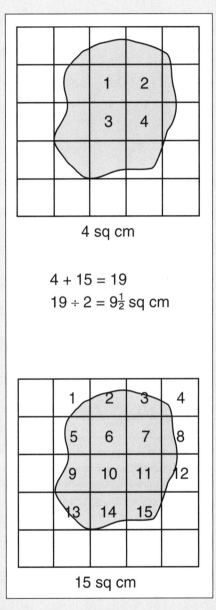

4 sq cm

$$4 + 15 = 19$$
$$19 \div 2 = 9\tfrac{1}{2} \text{ sq cm}$$

15 sq cm

Figure 13: *One method for estimating the area of an irregular shape*

Estimates for the Area of Shape __1__

Median = __16 sq cm__

Name	Estimate
Manny	17 sq cm
Lee Yah	16 sq cm
Shannon	14 sq cm
Jerome	16 sq cm

Estimates for the Area of Shape __6__

Median = __82 sq cm__

Name	Estimate
Alexis	81 sq cm
Arti	83 sq cm
Michael	72 sq cm
Brandon	82 sq cm
John	$86\frac{1}{2}$ sq cm

Figure 14: *Group members share their estimates by recording their data in a table.*

Content Note

Outliers in Data. When scientists see a measurement that is very different from the rest of the data, they may suspect that something went wrong with that measurement. In these cases, they sometimes, "throw out" that measurement when they analyze their data. Often they replace the measurement by taking another trial. The low estimate of 72 sq cm for Shape 6, for example, could be thrown out since it seems unreasonable in comparison to the other pieces of data.

When all groups finish their data collection, ask for the group assigned to Shape 6 to volunteer to share their measurements for their assigned shape. Transfer their data onto the board or onto a transparency of a *Two-column Data Table.*

The following discussion prompts use the estimates in the data table for Shape 6 in Figure 14 as examples. Use the prompts to help guide a discussion on what it means to be close using your students' data on one of the shapes. Tell students that we cannot find the exact area of each irregular shape. By finding the median estimate, we average out the errors in our measurement. We assume the median is our best estimate of the actual measurement. In this case, using our sample data in Figure 14, the median, or our best estimate for Shape 6, is 82 sq cm. Ask:

*   *Whose estimates match the median exactly?* (One or two of the students' estimates might match the median. It is less likely for larger areas like Shape 6 than for smaller shapes such as Shapes 1 and 2.)

- *Whose estimates are close to the median for Shape 6?* (More students will be able to say that their estimates are close.)

- *Which estimates are close enough to the median to be good estimates? How much larger or smaller can your estimate be and still be a good estimate?* (Let students choose a range of values that makes sense to them. They may say that the estimates must be within 5 square centimeters to be close. Any reasonable range will do for now. For example, if the median estimate for Shape 6's area is 82 sq cm, then students may choose to accept estimates in the range of 77 to 87 sq cm.)

Ask a second group that was assigned to a small shape such as Shape 1 or 2 to volunteer. Ask:

- *Whose estimates match the median exactly?*

- *Whose estimates are close?*

- *Which estimates are close enough to the median to be good estimates? How much larger or smaller can your estimate be and still be a good estimate?* (At first, students may choose the same range of values as they did for the larger shape. For example, if the median estimate for Shape 1 is 16 sq cm, students may say that good estimates may also be within 5 sq cm of the median estimate. However, other students may feel that estimates as low as 11 sq cm and as high as 21 sq cm are not good estimates for Shape 1.)

- *Do you think it is fair to judge our estimates for both the large and small shapes using the same standard?* (Students should begin to see that the larger the shape, the larger the range of acceptable estimates and the smaller the shape, the smaller the range of acceptable values. It is clear that we cannot use a difference of 5 sq cm as our standard for both Shapes 1 and 6. Estimates within 5 sq cm of 82 sq cm for Shape 6, such as 77– 87 sq cm, can be considered good estimates. However, using the same standard for acceptable estimates for the number of sq cm in Shape 1 is not appropriate.)

- *If there are 474 students in the school, is an estimate of 500 students close enough?* (In many situations, yes. Note: The difference between the actual number of students and the estimate is 26 students.)

- *If there are 27 students in the classroom, is an estimate within 26 (between 1 and 53) close enough?* (Obviously, no. Note: The difference between the actual number of students in the class and this "estimate" is also 26 students.)

Content Note

Accuracy and Precision in Measurement. The accuracy required in a measurement depends on the use we are going to make of the measurement. Any measurement we make in the real world is an estimation. If we measure the length and width of a rectangle to be 5.1 cm and 4.2 cm, we could say the area is 21.4 sq cm. If the rectangle is really closer to 5.14 cm than 5.1 cm, we could not tell this with our ruler, since it is only divided into tenths of a centimeter. So, in this example, the measurements we make are really estimates that are accurate to the nearest tenth of a centimeter. For our purposes, a measurement of 21.4 sq cm is probably more than sufficient.

If the measurement we make for a shape with straight sides such as a rectangle is, in actuality, an estimation, how then can we find the actual area of an irregular shape? We cannot. We can estimate by counting whole square centimeters and by piecing fractional units together to form more whole square centimeters. We can take several trials and cancel out possible errors in our work by finding the average or median value of the set of data. Then, we can assume the median estimate is our best estimate. See the TIMS Tutor: *Estimation, Accuracy, and Error* for a more detailed discussion on making estimates and deciding if estimates are "close enough."

Using 10% as a Standard. We want a standard that gives us a larger range for larger numbers than for smaller numbers. One way to do this is to use percent. For most measurements in *Math Trailblazers,* we will say that "close enough" means "within 10%." That is, an estimate is "close enough" if it is within 10% of the actual number. Since we cannot find the actual area of these irregular shapes, we compare the estimates of a shape to the median estimate— our best estimate. Ten percent means 10 out of every 100 or 1 out of every 10. Therefore, for every 10 square centimeters in a shape, an estimate can be off by 1 square centimeter and still be considered accurate for our purposes.

Use the following prompts to discuss **ten percent** (10%) of a number. You can choose one of the shapes as an example. The prompts here use the sample data for Shape 1 in Figure 14. Students will need calculators.

- *The median estimate for Shape 1 is 16 sq cm; 100% means one whole or all the square centimeters. How many square centimeters is 100% of the area?* (16 sq cm)

- *Fifty percent means 50 out of 100 or $\frac{1}{2}$. About how many square centimeters is 50% of the area?* (About 8 sq cm)

- *Ten percent means 10 out of every 100 or $\frac{1}{10}$. One way to find 10% or $\frac{1}{10}$ of the square centimeters is to divide by 10. What is $\frac{1}{10}$ or 10% of 16?* (Between 1 and 2. About 2.)

- *We can use division to find 10% of a number or $\frac{1}{10}$ of a number. Use your calculator to divide 16 by 10. What shows on your display?* (1.6)

- *Ten percent of 16 is about what number?* (2. To show students that 1.6 is close to 2, use a centimeter ruler as a number line. Locate 1.6 cm on a centimeter ruler and ask students to find the closest whole centimeter.)

- *About how low can your estimate be and still be within 10% of the median estimate for Shape 1? What is 10% less than 16?* (16 − 2 = 14 sq cm)

- *About how high can your estimate be and still be within 10% of the median? What is 10% more than 16?* (16 + 2 = 18 sq cm)

- *So, what is the range of numbers that are within 10% of 16? What is the lowest reasonable estimate? What is the highest?* (14 sq cm to 18 sq cm)

- *Look at the data table for Shape 1. Their median estimate is 16 sq cm. Whose estimates are within 10% of the median?*

Content Note

Why 10%? Using 10% as a benchmark is not always appropriate. If carpenters made errors as large as 10% of their specifications when making doors, many doors would not close. However, for classroom purposes 10% is a good standard for the following reasons:

1. It's easy to find 10%, or at least to estimate it.

2. In many of the hands-on experiments students do, 10% is about the accuracy we can expect from students using the equipment they have, while 10% accuracy is still good enough for seeing patterns in data on graphs.

3. Psychologically, 10% is near the limit of our visual estimating ability. For example, if you show a person two drawings in sequence—one an enlargement of the other—in most cases that person will have difficulty distinguishing pictures that are less than 10% different in size. For more information, see the TIMS Tutor: *Estimation, Accuracy, and Error* in the *Teacher Implementation Guide.*

Make a class data table using a transparency of the *10% Chart* in the *Discovery Assignment Book* or make a large class data table with the same headings on easel paper as shown in Figure 15. Tell students to use their copies of the *10% Chart* Activity Page and fill in the first row of the table with the appropriate information for the shape you used in your discussion. The data for Shapes 1 and 6 are used as examples here.

10% Chart

Shape	*M* Median Estimate	*M* ÷ 10 (Calculated)	10% of the Median (Estimated)	Range
1	16 sq cm	1.6	About 2	14–18 sq cm
6	82 sq cm	8.2	About 8	74–90 sq cm

Figure 15: *Sample 10% Chart*

Choose another shape and calculate 10% of the median by using mental math or calculators. Fill in the data table with the appropriate information. Since we only need an approximation of 10%, we can round or truncate the values in the third column (M ÷ 10, Calculated) to find the values in the fourth column (10% of the Median, Estimated).

You may wish to continue filling in the *10% Chart* as a whole class. Students can work with you and fill in their own copies of the chart. Or, you can fill in the first two columns on the class chart to give students the median estimates from each group. Then, groups can complete several rows and report their results to the whole class.

As you fill in the table, ask students to look for patterns. Students should see that they can often get a pretty good estimate for 10% of a whole number by dropping the ones digit. If students are familiar with decimals, remind them that a decimal point follows any whole number (e.g., 16 is the same as 16.0). Therefore, dividing a number by 10 results in moving the decimal point one place to the left. To approximate 10% of a number, students can round or truncate this quotient.

- *What happens to the range of acceptable estimates as the shapes get larger?* (The range gets larger.)
- *What happens to the range when the shapes get smaller?* (The range gets smaller.)

Discovery Assignment Book - page 65

Student Guide - page 118

Student Guide - page 119 *(Answers on p. 94)*

Student Guide - page 120 *(Answers on p. 94)*

Part 2 When Are Estimates Close Enough?

After students complete the table, they are ready to discuss the questions in the *Student Guide.* In pairs, students can read the introduction and complete *Questions 1–11.* Alternatively, you may read the introduction together as a class and discuss *Questions 1–7* together. Students can then complete the rest of the *Student Guide* pages in pairs and come together as a class to discuss their answers to *Questions 8–11.*

Questions 1–2 ask students to identify the median of two sets of data. *Questions 3–6* ask students to compare individual estimates of the area of two shapes to the median estimate.

Question 7 reviews the notion of relative error: when the median estimate for the area of a shape is 42 sq cm, then 45 sq cm is a pretty good estimate. But, when the median estimate for the area of a shape is 10 sq cm, 7 sq cm is not as good an estimate. Although in both cases the difference between the median and the estimate is 3 sq cm, the error should be smaller when the area is smaller.

The text and questions following *Question 7* in the *Student Guide* review the use of 10% as a guideline for deciding which estimates are "close enough." Two methods for finding 10% of a number are discussed: using mental math to find one-tenth and using a calculator to divide by 10. Students may prefer other methods.

Using the example of a shape that has a median estimate of 10 sq cm, *Question 8* asks for estimates that are within 10% of 10. Since Felicia's, Lin's, and Irma's estimates of 9 sq cm, 10 sq cm, and 11 sq cm are within the range of 9 to 11 sq cm, their estimates are within 10% of the median. However, Shannon's and Roberto's estimates of 7 and 16 sq cm are outside the range, so their estimates are not within 10% of the median.

Roberto's high estimate of 16 sq cm is not considered a close estimate. Students may have expected this at the start, before any calculations were completed. The difference between Roberto's estimate and the second highest estimate of 11 sq cm is 5 sq cm. This difference makes his data somewhat questionable. Also, look at his method for estimating the area of Shape A in the *Student Guide.* You can see his estimate of 16 sq cm is "way off." He enclosed Shape A within a square. The square's area is much greater than Shape A. If you regard Roberto's estimate as

unreasonable, and find the median of the remaining four pieces of data, instead of all five, the median is $9\frac{1}{2}$ sq cm instead of 10 sq cm. Both $9\frac{1}{2}$ sq cm and 10 sq cm represent the data equally well. When using the median, the need to throw out unreasonable pieces of data is not imperative since the median will eliminate the high and low estimates anyway.

Question 9 repeats the process using the median estimate for another shape. Students can first find 10% of 42. If they use a calculator to divide 42 by 10, the display will show 4.2. With some discussion they can see that 4.2 is between 4 and 5, and closer to 4. Arti, Romesh, and Lee Yah made estimates within 10% of 42 sq cm, but Nicholas and Nila did not. Before making any calculations, we may consider the low estimate of 36 sq cm and the high estimate of 49 sq cm as unreasonable estimates. They both seem to be "way off." If we throw these two pieces of data out and find the median of the remaining three pieces of data, we would find that the median would still be 42 sq cm. Again, using the median eliminates the gross errors in the data.

Question 10 provides more practice finding 10% of a number and identifying estimates which are within 10%. Give the class an opportunity to repeat the estimation process using different shapes. Be sure to add these numbers to the class *10% Chart* and continue to analyze the pattern in the chart.

Question 11 asks students to use number sense to determine which estimates for Shape D might be questionable, or might be worth disregarding. Students might decide that 80 sq cm and 100 sq cm seem unreasonable in comparison to the other pieces of data. Whether they find the median value of all five pieces of data or only three or four, students will see that the median is not affected greatly.

Journal Prompt

How can you find 10% of a number? Describe all the ways you know.

Homework and Practice

Assign the Homework section on the *How Close Is Close Enough?* Activity Pages in the *Student Guide*.

---

9. Look back at the estimates for Shape B. Which estimates are within 10% of the median? Is Arti's?

10. Answer the following questions using the data for Shape C.
   A. What is the median estimate for Shape C?
   B. What is 10% of the median?
   C. What is the range of estimates that are within 10% of the median?
   D. Which estimates are within 10% of the median?
   E. Which estimates are not within 10% of the median?

Shape C

Name	Estimate
Manny	32 sq cm
Blanca	31 sq cm
Michael	32 sq cm
Jackie	42 sq cm
Ana	28 sq cm
Edward	35 sq cm

11. Below is the data table for Shape D. Answer the following questions using this set of data.
   A. What is the median estimate?
   B. Look at the data. Compare the five estimates. Do any of the estimates seem unreasonable? Would you consider throwing out any of the data? If so, which one or ones?
   C. Take out the pieces of data that seem "way off." Now, find the median of the remaining data. Do the high and low estimates affect the median very much? Explain.

Shape D

Name	Estimate
Frank	91 sq cm
Brandon	86 sq cm
David	100 sq cm
Jessie	80 sq cm
John	88 sq cm

Student Guide - page 121 (Answers on p. 95)

Homework

1. Frank drew a shape with curved sides on *Centimeter Grid Paper*. Each student in the class estimated its area. The class's median estimate for Frank's shape is 51 sq cm. Is an estimate of 60 sq cm within 10% of the median estimate for the area of Frank's shape? Show how you know.

2. Brandon drew a shape, too. The class's median estimate for his shape is 103 sq cm. Is an estimate of 115 square centimeters within 10% of the median estimate for the area of Brandon's shape? Show how you know.

3. Before completing the *Distance vs. Time* lab in Unit 2, Jessie predicted that she could walk about 20 yards in 10 seconds. After completing the lab, she found that she actually walked 15 yards in 10 seconds. Is her prediction of 20 yards within 10% of the actual distance of 15 yards? Why or why not?

4. Mr. Moreno brought in a jar filled with pennies. Felicia estimated that the jar contained 215 pennies. There were actually 198 pennies in the jar. Is Felicia's estimate within 10% of the actual number of pennies in the jar?

5. On a television game show, contestants win a prize if they guess the price within 10% of the actual price. If a television costs $225, what is the range of winning guesses?

6. On the same game show, a new car is offered as a prize. A contestant estimates the price of the car to be $15,000. The actual price is $14,500. Does the contestant win the prize? How do you know?

7. Brandon's sister Becky is a waitress at a restaurant. She received a 10% tip on a customer's bill. If she received a $2 tip, what was the customer's bill?

8. One of Becky's customers wants to leave a 20% tip. If his bill is $16, how much should he leave? (*Hint:* Find 10% of the bill first.)

Student Guide - page 122 (Answers on p. 95)

Part 1. Estimating the Area of an Irregular Shape

1. Students work in groups of 3 or 4. Assign each group one of the shapes on *Shapes 1–5* or *Shapes 6 and 7* Activity Pages. Each student estimates the area of the shape assigned to his or her group.

2. Students record their estimates in a d ata table. The group finds the median estimate and records this on the table as well.

3. Use the discussion prompts to guide a discussion on what it means to have a close estimate.

4. Establish a general standard for closeness: An estimated area is close if it is within 10% of the median estimate, the best estimate we have.

5. Use the discussion prompts to describe how to find 10% of a number.

6. The class completes the *10% Chart* Activity Page in the *Discovery Assignment Book* to practice finding 10%. Students use the chart to look for patterns to help them find 10% easily.

Part 2. When Are Estimates Close Enough?

1. Students review and practice skills and concepts from Part 1 by discussing *Questions 1–11* on the *How Close Is Close Enough?* Activity Pages in the *Student Guide*.

2. Students repeat the estimation process using different shapes. (optional)

Homework

Assign the Homework section in the *Student Guide*.

Answer Key is on pages 94–96.

Notes:

Shapes 1–5

Estimate the area of your assigned shape. Record your group's estimates in a data table.

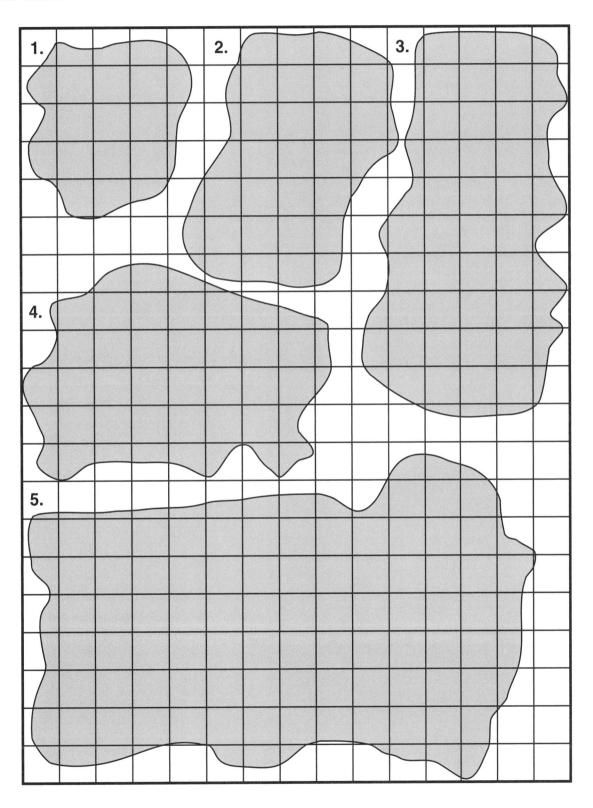

Shapes 6 and 7

Estimate the area of your assigned shape. Record your group's estimates in a data table.

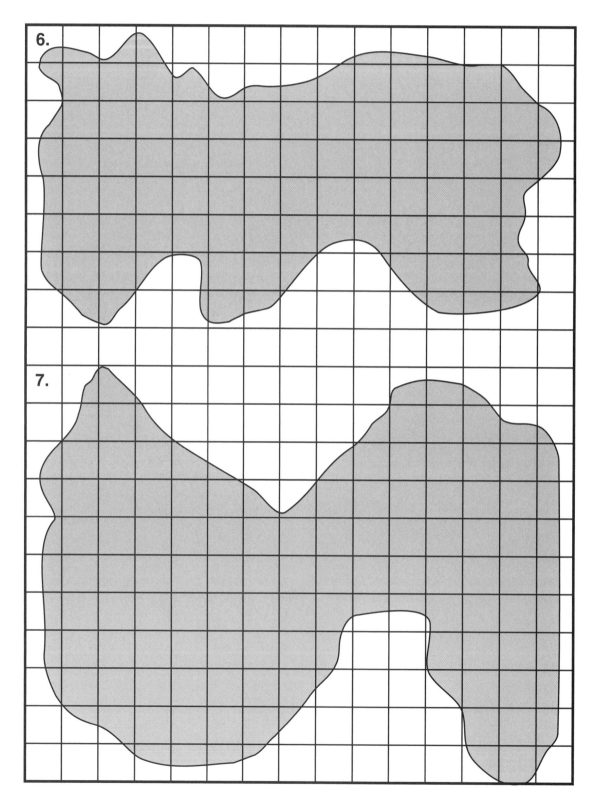

Name _____   Date _____

_____

Two-column Data Table, Blackline Master

Mr. Moreno overheard their conversation. He said to the class, "Felicia and Roberto have a good question. How accurate can the measurements of an irregular shape be? How close is close enough?"

He gave each student a copy of an irregular shape that was traced on *Centimeter Grid Paper*. He asked each student to find the area of the shape in square centimeters. Felicia, Roberto, and the three other students in their group estimate the area of Shape A. Felicia's and Roberto's work is shown below.

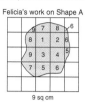 Felicia's work on Shape A

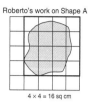 Roberto's work on Shape A

9 sq cm

4 × 4 = 16 sq cm

The members in Felicia and Roberto's group compare their estimates. They each record their own measurement in a data table. Five other students measure a different shape, Shape B. Here are the estimates for Shape A and Shape B.

Shape A

Name	Estimate
Lin	10 sq cm
Felicia	9 sq cm
Shannon	7 sq cm
Roberto	16 sq cm
Irma	11 sq cm

Shape B

Name	Estimate
Arti	45 sq cm
Romesh	42 sq cm
Lee Yah	42 sq cm
Nicholas	49 sq cm
Nila	36 sq cm

1. What is the median estimate for Shape A? How do you know?
2. What is the median estimate for Shape B? How do you know?

Student Guide - page 119

3. What is the difference between Shannon's estimate and the median estimate for Shape A?
4. What is the difference between Felicia's estimate for Shape A and the median estimate?
5. What is the difference between Lee Yah's estimate and the median estimate for Shape B?
6. What is the difference between Arti's estimate for Shape B and the median estimate?
7. Is Shannon's estimate for Shape A better, worse, or the same as Arti's estimate for Shape B? Explain.

Mr. Moreno said, "Let's say that an estimate is close enough if it's within ten percent of the actual value. We don't know the exact area of these irregular shapes. We'll assume that the median of each is our best estimate. We'll say the other estimates are close enough if they are within 10% of the median. **Ten percent** (10%) means 10 out of every 100. That's the same as 1 out of every 10 or $\frac{1}{10}$. Let's find out what 10% of the median estimate for Shape A is. The median estimate is 10 sq cm, so 10% or $\frac{1}{10}$ of 10 is 1."

Ten percent of 10 is 1, so 10% less than 10 is 9 and 10% more than 10 is 11. Thus, any estimate in the range between 9 and 11 is within 10% of 10.

8. **A.** Look back at the estimates for Shape A. Which estimates are within 10% of the median?
   B. Which estimates are not within 10% of the median?

Mr. Moreno said, "Now let's find 10% of the median estimate for Shape B. The median estimate is 42 sq cm. How can we find 10% of 42?"

Felicia estimates $\frac{1}{10}$ of 42 in her head. She says, "42 ÷ 10 is about 4."

Romesh uses a calculator to find $\frac{1}{10}$ of 42. He divides 42 by 10. Since the display reads 4.2, he agrees with Felicia that 10% of 42 is about 4.

Any estimate in the range between 38 and 46 is within 10% of 42, since:

42 − 4 = 38
and
42 + 4 = 46.

Student Guide - page 120

Student Guide (p. 119)

1. 10 sq cm
2. 42 sq cm

Student Guide (p. 120)

3. 3 sq cm
4. 1 sq cm
5. 0 sq cm
6. 3 sq cm
7. From the discussion in Part 1 of the lesson students should argue that Arti's is better since the area she counted was larger.*
8. **A.** Felicia's, Lin's, and Irma's estimates are within 10% of the median.*

   B. Shannon's and Roberto's estimates are not within 10% of the median.

*Answers and/or discussion are included in the Lesson Guide.

Student Guide (p. 121)

9. Lee Yah's, Romesh's, and Arti's estimates are within 10% of the median. Yes.*

10. A. 32 sq cm

  B. 3.2, between 3 and 4; 3

  C. 29–35 sq cm

  D. Manny's, Blanca's, Michael's, and Edward's estimates are within 10% of the median.

  E. Ana's and Jackie's estimates are not within 10% of the median.

11.* A. 88 sq cm

  B. 100 sq cm or 80 and 100 sq cm

  C. If students decide to throw out only 100 sq cm, the median of the remaining four pieces of data is 87 sq cm. If students decide to throw out 80 sq cm and 100 sq cm, then the median of the remaining three pieces is 88 sq cm. No. The high and low estimates do not figure in the median.

---

9. Look back at the estimates for Shape B. Which estimates are within 10% of the median? Is Arti's?

10. Answer the following questions using the data for Shape C.
  A. What is the median estimate for Shape C?
  B. What is 10% of the median?
  C. What is the range of estimates that are within 10% of the median?
  D. Which estimates are within 10% of the median?
  E. Which estimates are not within 10% of the median?

Shape C

Name	Estimate
Manny	32 sq cm
Blanca	31 sq cm
Michael	32 sq cm
Jackie	42 sq cm
Ana	28 sq cm
Edward	35 sq cm

11. Below is the data table for Shape D. Answer the following questions using this set of data.
  A. What is the median estimate?
  B. Look at the data. Compare the five estimates. Do any of the estimates seem unreasonable? Would you consider throwing out any of the data? If so, which one or ones?
  C. Take out the pieces of data that seem "way off." Now, find the median of the remaining data. Do the high and low estimates affect the median very much? Explain.

Shape D

Name	Estimate
Frank	91 sq cm
Brandon	86 sq cm
David	100 sq cm
Jessie	80 sq cm
John	88 sq cm

Student Guide - page 121

Student Guide (p. 122)

Homework

1. No. Ten percent of 51 is about 5. Estimates within 10% of the median are those from 46 sq cm to 56 sq cm. 60 sq cm is out of this range.

2. No. Ten percent of 103 sq cm is about 10 sq cm. Estimates within 10% of the median are those from 93 to 113 sq cm; 115 sq cm is a bit high.

3. No, the 10% range is 13.5 yards–16.5 yards; 20 yards does not fall within the range.

4. Yes, the 10% range is 178 pennies–218 pennies; 215 pennies is within that range.

5. $202.50–$247.50

6. Estimates in the range of $13,050 and $15,950 are within 10% of the actual price. The contestant wins the car.

7. $20

8. $3.20

Homework

1. Frank drew a shape with curved sides on *Centimeter Grid Paper*. Each student in the class estimated its area. The class's median estimate for Frank's shape is 51 sq cm. Is an estimate of 60 sq cm within 10% of the median estimate for the area of Frank's shape? Show how you know.

2. Brandon drew a shape, too. The class's median estimate for his shape is 103 sq cm. Is an estimate of 115 square centimeters within 10% of the median estimate for the area of Brandon's shape? Show how you know.

3. Before completing the *Distance vs. Time* lab in Unit 2, Jessie predicted that she could walk about 20 yards in 10 seconds. After completing the lab, she found that she actually walked 15 yards in 10 seconds. Is her prediction of 20 yards within 10% of the actual distance of 15 yards? Why or why not?

4. Mr. Moreno brought in a jar filled with pennies. Felicia estimated that the jar contained 215 pennies. There were actually 198 pennies in the jar. Is Felicia's estimate within 10% of the actual number of pennies in the jar?

5. On a television game show, contestants win a prize if they guess the price within 10% of the actual price. If a television costs $225, what is the range of winning guesses?

6. On the same game show, a new car is offered as a prize. A contestant estimates the price of the car to be $15,000. The actual price is $14,500. Does the contestant win the prize? How do you know?

7. Brandon's sister Becky is a waitress at a restaurant. She received a 10% tip on a customer's bill. If she received a $2 tip, what was the customer's bill?

8. One of Becky's customers wants to leave a 20% tip. If his bill is $16, how much should he leave? (*Hint:* Find 10% of the bill first.)

Student Guide - page 122

*Answers and/or discussion are included in the Lesson Guide.

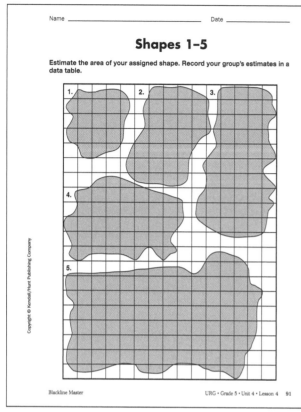

Unit Resource Guide - page 91

Unit Resource Guide (p. 91)

Shapes 1–5

One possible estimate is listed for each shape. As described in Lesson Guide 4, students find ranges of estimates that are within 10% of the median estimate.

1. About 16 sq cm
2. About 28 sq cm
3. About 44 sq cm
4. About 35 sq cm
5. About 90 sq cm

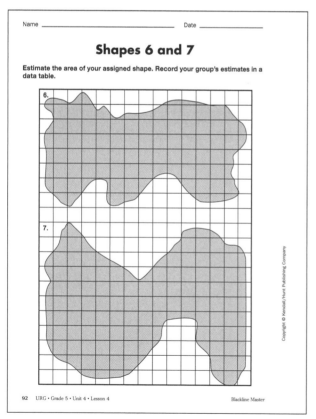

Unit Resource Guide - page 92

Unit Resource Guide (p. 92)

Shapes 6 and 7

One possible estimate is listed for each shape. As described in Lesson Guide 4, students find ranges of estimates that are within 10% of the median estimate.

6. 80 sq cm
7. 103 sq cm

Lesson 5

Mean or Median?

Estimated Class Sessions

2

Students review the mean as a different kind of average. Connecting cubes are used to model the mean as students even out towers that represent values of data. Students compare the mean and median. They review the order of operations and discuss parentheses.

Key Content

- Reviewing the concept of the mean.
- Comparing the mean and the median.
- Averaging: finding the median and mean.
- Using parentheses in numerical expressions.
- Using correct order of operations.

Key Vocabulary

- average
- mean
- numerical expression

Math Facts

Continue reviewing the multiplication and division facts for the square numbers.

Homework

Assign the Homework section in the *Student Guide.*

Assessment

Use DPP items Y and Z as quizzes.

Curriculum Sequence

Before This Unit

Finding the median value in experiments in *Math Trailblazers* began in first grade. The mean was introduced in Unit 5 Lesson 3 of fourth grade and used throughout fourth grade. Order of operations was introduced in Unit 7 of fourth grade.

After This Unit

Students will practice using the mean in various activities and labs throughout fifth grade. For example, they use the mean in the next lesson, *Spreading Out.* The mean is also used in the lab in Unit 5.

Materials List

Supplies and Copies

Student	Teacher
Supplies for Each Student • calculator **Supplies for Each Student Pair** • 80 connecting cubes or square-inch tiles	**Supplies**
Copies	**Copies/Transparencies**

All blackline masters including assessment, transparency, and DPP masters are also on the Teacher Resource CD.

Student Books

Mean or Median? (*Student Guide* Pages 123–130)

Daily Practice and Problems and Home Practice

DPP items O–R (*Unit Resource Guide* Pages 25–26)

Note: Classrooms whose pacing differs significantly from the suggested pacing of the units should use the Math Facts Calendar in Section 4 of the *Facts Resource Guide* to ensure students receive the complete math facts program.

O. Bit: Shortcut Division (URG p. 25)

Use a paper-and-pencil method to solve the following problems. Estimate to make sure your answers are reasonable.

A. 1739 ÷ 5

B. 467 ÷ 3

C. 1056 ÷ 6

Q. Bit: Reading Scientific Notation
(URG p. 26)

Shannon solves a problem on her calculator.

The answer to the problem is 6.2×10^9.

1. Write the answer in standard form.
2. Write the answer in words.

P. Challenge: Vacation Planning
(URG p. 25)

Arti's grandparents are planning a three-day vacation weekend to celebrate their 40th wedding anniversary. Here is a list of things they must consider when planning how much money they will need.

• They are staying at a hotel that includes breakfast and lunch for two for a total cost of $97 each night. They are staying at the hotel for three nights.

• They plan on tipping the maid 10% of the cost of the room for one night.

• They have to buy dinner for the three evenings for $13.95 a person.

• They plan on leaving a 20% tip at the restaurant each evening.

About how much money do they need to pay for this weekend get-away? Show all the steps in your solution.

R. Task: Estimation (URG p. 26)

Estimate the answers to the following problems. Then explain your thinking.

1. About how many 14s are in 150?
2. About how many 25s are in 280?
3. About how many 20s are in 312?
4. About how many 40s are in 2591?

Student Guide - page 123

Mean or Median?

Another Average: The Mean

Romesh is on the basketball team.

Here are the points he scored for the first five games.

Game	Points
Game #1	4
Game #2	6
Game #3	4
Game #4	23
Game #5	28

My median score is 6 points per game. I can say that is my average score. But, it doesn't really show my last two games when I scored a lot of points.

Remember, the average is one number that represents a typical value in a set of data. The median is the number that is exactly in the middle of the data. The median is often used as the average because it is easy to find. Another kind of average, called the mean, is also used. Sometimes the mean describes the data better.

Mean or Median?   SG • Grade 5 • Unit 4 • Lesson 5   **123**

Student Guide - page 123

Student Guide - page 124

To find Romesh's mean score, we can use connecting cubes.

1. **A.** For this problem, each connecting cube represents one point. How many connecting cubes do you need to represent all the points Romesh scored?

   B. Make 5 towers, one for each game. Use cubes to show the points Romesh scored during each game. Then divide the connecting cubes into 5 equal towers. Think of this as dividing all the points evenly among the five games.

Towers Showing   Romesh's Scores
Romesh's Scores   Evened Out

2. How many connecting cubes are in each tower?

Romesh's mean score is 13 points per game. We can say he averaged 13 points per game.

To find his mean points per game on a calculator, Romesh used the following keystrokes:

| 4 | + | 6 | + | 4 | + | 23 | + | 28 | = | ÷ | 5 | = |

He added his points and then divided by the number of games.

3. Which average—the mean or the median—do you think better describes Romesh's scores?

124 SG • Grade 5 • Unit 4 • Lesson 5   Mean or Median?

Student Guide - page 124 *(Answers on p. 106)*

Teaching the Activity

In Part 1 of this activity, students investigate the mean and compare it to the median. Part 2 focuses on order of operations and the use of parentheses in numerical expressions.

Part 1 Another Average: The Mean

TIMS Tip

This activity is described using connecting cubes. If your class does not have connecting cubes, use square-inch tiles instead. Where the activity asks students to build towers, students can make rows of square-inch tiles.

Use the *Mean or Median?* Activity Pages in the *Student Guide* to lead the discussion. The activity begins with Romesh finding his average points scored during 5 basketball games. Ask:

- *Why is Romesh unhappy with reporting an average of 6?*

Introduce the mean as another type of average. Remind students that an **average** is one number that represents a typical value in a set of numbers. Have students count out enough connecting cubes to represent the total number of points Romesh scored during the 5 games (65) for *Question 1.* Now, have students divide the cubes evenly into 5 towers. Each tower represents a game. Explain to students that we are evening out the points. We are looking for one number to represent all Romesh's scores. The number of cubes in each tower, when the towers are the same height, is the **mean.** In *Question 2,* students should find that each tower contains 13 cubes as shown in Figure 16.

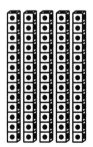

Towers Showing   Romesh's Scores
Romesh's Scores   Evened Out

Figure 16: *Evening out scores of 4, 6, 4, 23, and 28*

Thus, Romesh's mean score is 13 points per game. *Question 3* asks students to identify which number, the mean or the median, better represents Romesh's scores. The mean better reflects Romesh's efforts because while there are 3 scores well below 13, there are 2 scores well above 13.

Alternatively, you may wish to have students begin with the 5 towers that represent Romesh's scores (towers of 4, 6, 4, 23, and 28 cubes). Then, ask students to even out these towers so each tower has the same number of cubes.

Students should compute the mean using their calculators. Note that it is important to press ($=$) before dividing. Otherwise, the calculator may divide the last number entered, not the sum of the numbers. Show students how to avoid reentering all the data when they make a mistake. On many scientific calculators, a delete key (DEL) or back arrow key (←) allows correction of entered keystrokes. Advise students to follow the directions for their calculators.

Content Note

Median or Mean? For many sets of data, the median and the mean will be very close. In these cases, the choice of the mean or median depends on how easy it is to do the calculations. The median is often easier to find, and, for this reason, students have used it successfully to average data collected in labs in earlier grades. The mean is the most commonly used type of average and it often, although not always, represents data better than the median.

When calculating the mean, every value is involved in the computation. For example, in Romesh's basketball scores, the 4s and the 6 pulled Romesh's average down, but the 23 and the 28 pulled it up. The median often eliminates the high and low outliers. Romesh's median score is 6 because it is the middle value when the scores are ranked in order. See the TIMS Tutor: *Averages* in the *Teacher Implementation Guide* for a more detailed explanation of both the median and the mean and examples of situations when one is more appropriate to use than the other.

In *Questions 4–9,* students explore an example where the mean is not a whole number. When using the cubes, we can say that the average is more than 7, but less than 8. In *Question 7,* students find the mean to be 7.7 (to the nearest tenth) on their calculators. Since there is an even number of values, the median (7.5) is the value halfway between the two middle values. *(Question 8)* Students should see in *Question 9* that in this example, the mean and the median are very close. This often happens when the data are not very spread out.

The mean and the median are two kinds of averages. The **mean** for any data set is an average of numbers. It is found by adding the values of the data and dividing by the number of values.

There are 6 students in Irma's group. Here are the number of books they read in one month.

Student	Number of Books Read
Irma	8
Blanca	2
Arti	6
John	11
Lin	12
Edward	7

Find the mean number of books Irma's group read. Use connecting cubes.

4. How many connecting cubes do you need?
5. How many towers will you make?
6. What is the mean number of books?

It is impossible to give each tower an equal number of cubes. Each tower has at least 7 cubes. This tells us that the average is over 7, but less than 8.

7. Find the mean number of books Irma's group read. Use a calculator.
   A. What numbers did you add?
   B. What number did you divide by?

8. Find the median number of books Irma's group read.

9. How do the mean and the median compare?

Student Guide - page 125 (Answers on p. 106)

---

10. Shannon and Roberto's Social Studies teacher, Mrs. Smith, gives geography quizzes. Here are Shannon's and Roberto's quiz scores.

Shannon	3	9	9	2	9
Roberto	15	4	4	15	3

   A. Do you think Shannon would want Mrs. Smith to find her average using the mean or the median? Explain.
   B. Do you think Roberto would want Mrs. Smith to find his average using the mean or the median? Explain.

11. During winter break, Romesh and Alexis played a computer game. During the first game, Romesh got to level 5 while Alexis got to level 8. They kept track of how far they got in each game.

Game	Romesh's Level	Alexis's Level
Game 1	5	8
Game 2	10	2
Game 3	7	5
Game 4	3	18
Game 5	11	18
Game 6	14	8
Game 7	12	5
Game 8	10	16

Romesh says he found their averages and decided that he is the better player. Alexis says she found their averages, too. She claims that she is the better player. Can they both be right? Explain.

Student Guide - page 126 (Answers on p. 107)

12. Sometimes, the mean better describes the data. Other times, the median better describes the data. Here are yearly salaries at the Happy Day Manufacturing Company.

Position	Salary
President	$259,000
Vice-President	$123,000
Worker #1	$36,000
Worker #2	$25,000
Worker #3	$18,000
Worker #4	$32,000
Worker #5	$25,000
Worker #6	$22,000
Worker #7	$27,000

The president of the company announced that the average salary was $63,000 a year.

A. Is she correct?

B. Is the mean a good description of the data? Explain.

13. Last summer, Alexis swam the breaststroke in 5 swim meets. Her times are listed below.

56.6 seconds   51.3 seconds   44.8 seconds
47.5 seconds   45.8 seconds

A. Find her median time.

B. Use a calculator to find the mean.

Mean or Median? SG • Grade 5 • Unit 4 • Lesson 5 **127**

Student Guide - page 127 *(Answers on p. 107)*

---

14. Ana's group collected data for the lab *Distance vs. Time*. Jerome walked along a track. The rest of the group reported the time he took to walk 6 yards, 9 yards, and 12 yards. Ana was the timer at 6 yards. On the first trial she didn't know how to use the stopwatch. Here is the first row of their data table:

D Distance in Yards	T Time in Seconds			
	Trial 1	Trial 2	Trial 3	Average
6	10	3	5	

A. Find the mean value of the three trials.

B. Find the median value of the three trials.

C. Which average, the median or the mean, represents the data better? Explain your reasoning.

Order of Operations: Using Parentheses

Mr. Moreno showed the class another way to find averages on a calculator. If your calculator has ⬚(⬚ and ⬚)⬚ keys, try this method. The ⬚(⬚ and ⬚)⬚ are left and right parentheses. Parentheses are often used to show what operations to do first. For example, to find the mean number of points Romesh scored in the first 5 basketball games, we write (4 + 6 + 4 + 23 + 28) ÷ 5. Parentheses say do the work inside the parentheses first.

An example of a **numerical expression** is (4 + 6 + 4 + 23 + 28) ÷ 5. Numerical expressions have numbers and operations. In numerical expressions, we follow the order of operations. That is, we divide and multiply and then add and subtract. When there are parentheses in an expression, we do the calculations inside the parentheses first.

Since we multiply and divide before adding and subtracting,

3 × 2 + 5 = 11   6 ÷ 2 × 4 + 3 = 15
3 + 2 × 5 = 13   8 − 6 ÷ 3 + 4 = 10

15. Find the values of the following expressions.

A. 5 + 8 ÷ 4   **B.** 18 ÷ 3 + 4 × 7

C. 17 − 14 ÷ 2 − 3   **D.** 6 × 4 ÷ 3 − 2

128 SG • Grade 5 • Unit 4 • Lesson 5   Mean or Median?

Student Guide - page 128 *(Answers on p. 108)*

TIMS Tip

Students will encounter decimals when using a calculator to compute means. Depending on the data, they may ignore the decimal part (or remainder if using integer division) and use only the whole number part of the answer. In other situations, it is better to round to the closest whole number or closest tenth. Reminding students of money often helps. If the mean on the calculator shows 8.65, this can be rounded to 9 or to 8.7 since $8.65 is close to $9.00 or to $8.70. If you use the integer division function on your calculator, you can round up if the remainder is greater than half the divisor.

Questions 10–13 introduce the idea that using different kinds of averages sometimes results in different interpretations. And, people sometimes choose which to use, the mean or the median, to their advantage.

In *Question 10,* while Shannon's mean score is only 6.4, her median score is 9. On the other hand, Roberto's mean is 8.2 and his median is 4. Thus, Shannon would like the teacher to use the median, while Roberto would like the teacher to use the mean.

Question 12 brings up the important idea that sometimes the mean and other times the median better describes the data. Since most employees earn a salary in the 20–30 thousand dollar range, the median is more appropriate. The outliers (the president and the vice-president salaries) raise the mean value so much that it does not fairly represent the salaries of most employees.

Question 13 asks students to compute a mean involving decimal data. Allow students to use calculators and discuss whether they think the mean should be rounded or left as is. Since the times were reported with 1 decimal place, it is appropriate to leave the answer as 49.2 seconds.

Question 14 asks students to decide which average to use to represent data collected in an experiment. Students will have to make similar decisions in the next lesson in the lab *Spreading Out*. The data in this question refers to the lab *Distance vs. Time*. For one distance, a group recorded times of 10 seconds, 3 seconds, and 5 seconds. In this case, the median of 5 seconds better represents the data since it is not affected by the extreme value of 10 seconds. Alternatively, students can choose to throw out 10 seconds and find the average of the two remaining values. The best alternative is to collect more data.

Assign Homework *Questions 1–6* on the *Mean or Median?* Activity Pages in the *Student Guide.*

Part 2 **Order of Operations: Using Parentheses**

Use the *Student Guide* to introduce the use of parentheses in the context of calculating averages on a calculator. Explain that parentheses are often used in numerical expressions, and many people use them to do calculations on calculators. In any expression, the calculations inside the parentheses must be done first. A **numerical expression** is a combination of numbers and number operations.

For example, in the expression $(4 + 6) \div 5$, we first compute $4 + 6 = 10$. Then, we can eliminate the parentheses so the problem becomes $10 \div 5 = 2$. Remind students of the correct order of operations in expressions without parentheses: multiplication and division are done before addition and subtraction. Tell students to multiply and divide from left to right and then add and subtract from left to right when evaluating expressions.

Practice evaluating the expressions provided in the *Student Guide* in class together to make sure students understand the order of operations and working with parentheses.

Assign Homework *Questions 7–22* on the *Mean or Median?* Activity Pages in the *Student Guide.*

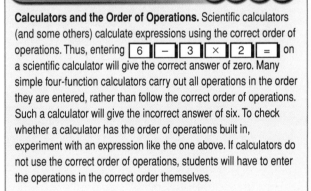

Content Note

Calculators and the Order of Operations. Scientific calculators (and some others) calculate expressions using the correct order of operations. Thus, entering ⬚6⬚ ⬚−⬚ ⬚3⬚ ⬚×⬚ ⬚2⬚ ⬚=⬚ on a scientific calculator will give the correct answer of zero. Many simple four-function calculators carry out all operations in the order they are entered, rather than follow the correct order of operations. Such a calculator will give the incorrect answer of six. To check whether a calculator has the order of operations built in, experiment with an expression like the one above. If calculators do not use the correct order of operations, students will have to enter the operations in the correct order themselves.

Work in parentheses must be done first. For example,

Example A. $3 + 6 \div 3 = 5$ Example B. $5 \times 4 + 2 = 22$
$(3 + 6) \div 3 = 3$ $5 \times (4 + 2) = 30$

16. First, find the values of the following expressions without a calculator. Then, use a calculator to check your work.

   A. $3 \times (12 - 6) =$ **B.** $3 \times 12 - 6 =$
   C. $(6 + 3) \times (5 - 2) =$ **D.** $6 + 3 \times 5 - 2 =$
   E. $16 \div 4 - 2 =$ **F.** $16 \div (4 - 2) =$
   G. $100 \div 10 - 5 =$ **H.** $100 \div (10 - 5) =$

Homework

1. Mr. Moreno's class recorded the daily high and low temperatures in degrees Fahrenheit for 5 days:

Temperature	Monday	Tuesday	Wednesday	Thursday	Friday
High	52°F	38°F	40°F	35°F	48°F
Low	35°F	28°F	30°F	32°F	43°F

   A. Find the mean high for the 5 days.
   B. Find the mean low for the 5 days.

2. Jessie went bowling with her friends. The first game she bowled 125 points. The second game she bowled 110 points. The third game she bowled 130 points. What was her average score that day? Use the mean.

3. Jessie's team bowled 3 games each. Each team member added their scores for their three games. The totals for the players on her team were 365, 352, 289, and 299. What was the average score for the 4 players on Jessie's team?

4. The heights of 5 players on a basketball team are: 195 cm, 202 cm, 207 cm, 201 cm, and 198 cm.
   A. What is the mean height in cm?
   B. Estimate the average height in inches. (*Hint:* 100 cm is about 39 in.)
   C. Express your answer to Question 4B in feet and inches.

5. Blanca's mother drove a total of 330 miles in 6 hours. What was her mean speed in miles per hour?

Mean or Median?   SG • Grade 5 • Unit 4 • Lesson 5   **129**

Student Guide - page 129 *(Answers on p. 108)*

---

6. Felicia's piano teacher has 8 students. Each student plays a song in the piano recital. The ages of the students are 7, 48, 10, 10, 11, 11, 6, and 9 years old.
   A. Find the mean age of the students.
   B. Find the median age.
   C. If you can only use one number to represent the ages of the students in the recital, which value would you use—the mean or the median? Explain.

Find the value of the following expressions. Do not use a calculator. Then use a calculator to check your answers.

  7. $6 + 3 \times 2 =$ 8. $12 \div 2 - 3 =$
  9. $7 \times 4 + 3 =$ 10. $10 - 2 \times 3 =$
11. $32 + 30 \div 10 =$ 12. $5 - 5 \div 5 \times 5 + 5 =$
13. $50 - 9 \div 3 =$ 14. $18 - 4 \div 2 \times 6 =$
15. $(50 + 4) \div 9 =$ 16. $17 - 20 \div 10 =$
17. $12 \div (6 \div 2) =$ 18. $(6 + 3) \times (7 - 4) =$
19. $12 \div (11 - 6 + 1) =$ 20. $28 \div (11 - 6 + 2) =$
21. $(17 + 4) \div 3 =$ 22. $17 - (64 \div 8) \times 2 =$

130   SG • Grade 5 • Unit 4 • Lesson 5   Mean or Median?

Student Guide - page 130 *(Answers on p. 109)*

Homework and Practice

- Homework is provided on the *Mean or Median?* Activity Pages in the *Student Guide.* You can assign *Questions 1–6* after Part 1 of this activity and *Questions 7–22* after Part 2.

- Assign DPP items O, Q, and R, which provide practice with division, scientific notation, and estimation.

Assessment

You can use two DPP items for subsequent lessons as short quizzes. Use item Y as a quiz on means and medians and item Z as a quiz on order of operations.

Extension

Assign DPP Challenge P, which provides a series of problems involving money and practice finding 10% of a number. This item is appropriate for students who have completed optional Lesson 4 *How Close Is Close Enough?*

Math Facts and Daily Practice and Problems

Assign DPP items O–R and continue reviewing the multiplication and division facts for the square numbers.

Part 1. Another Average: The Mean

1. Use the Another Average: The Mean section on the *Mean or Median?* Activity Pages in the *Student Guide* to introduce the mean as another type of average.
2. Discuss why Romesh is unhappy to report an average score of 6 points per game.
3. Model finding Romesh's mean score by evening out towers of connecting cubes. *(Questions 1–2)*
4. Generalize finding the mean of a set of values by adding the values and dividing by the number of values.
5. Discuss finding the mean on a calculator.
6. Students complete *Questions 3–14* in the *Student Guide.*

Part 2. Order of Operations: Using Parentheses

1. Use the *Mean or Median?* Activity Pages in the *Student Guide* to introduce the use of parentheses.
2. Review the order of operations: multiplication and division before addition and subtraction. Examples are provided.
3. Explain that computations inside parentheses are done first. Provide examples or use the examples in the *Student Guide.*

Homework

Assign the Homework section in the *Student Guide.*

Assessment

Use DPP items Y and Z as quizzes.

Extension

Assign DPP Challenge P.

Answer Key is on pages 106–109.

Notes:

To find Romesh's mean score, we can use connecting cubes.

1. **A.** For this problem, each connecting cube represents one point. How many connecting cubes do you need to represent all the points Romesh scored?

   B. Make 5 towers, one for each game. Use cubes to show the points Romesh scored during each game. Then divide the connecting cubes into 5 equal towers. Think of this as dividing all the points evenly among the five games.

Towers Showing
Romesh's Scores

Romesh's Scores
Evened Out

2. How many connecting cubes are in each tower?

Romesh's mean score is 13 points per game. We can say he averaged 13 points per game.

To find his mean points per game on a calculator, Romesh used the following keystrokes:

| 4 | + | 6 | + | 4 | + | 23 | + | 28 | = | ÷ | 5 | = |

He added his points and then divided by the number of games.

3. Which average—the mean or the median—do you think better describes Romesh's scores?

Student Guide - page 124

The mean and the median are two kinds of averages. The **mean** for any data set is an average of numbers. It is found by adding the values of the data and dividing by the number of values.

There are 6 students in Irma's group. Here are the number of books they read in one month.

Student	Number of Books Read
Irma	8
Blanca	2
Arti	6
John	11
Lin	12
Edward	7

Find the mean number of books Irma's group read. Use connecting cubes.

4. How many connecting cubes do you need?

5. How many towers will you make?

6. What is the mean number of books?

It is impossible to give each tower an equal number of cubes. Each tower has at least 7 cubes. This tells us that the average is over 7, but less than 8.

7. Find the mean number of books Irma's group read. Use a calculator.
   A. What numbers did you add?
   B. What number did you divide by?

8. Find the median number of books Irma's group read.

9. How do the mean and the median compare?

Student Guide - page 125

*Answers and/or discussion are included in the Lesson Guide.

Student Guide (p. 124)

1.* **A.** 65 cubes

   B. See Figure 16 in Lesson Guide 5.

2. 13 cubes*

3. the mean*

Student Guide (p. 125)

4. 46 cubes*

5. 6 towers

6. Between 7–8 books*

7. Rounding to the nearest tenth gives us 7.7 books.*

   A. 8, 2, 6, 11, 12, and 7

   B. 6

8. $7\frac{1}{2}$ books*

9. They are very close.*

Student Guide (p. 126)

10.* A. Median. Shannon's mean score is 6.4 and her median score is 9. The median gives a higher score.

B. Mean. Roberto's mean score is 8.2 and his median score is 4. The mean gives the higher score.

11. Romesh's median is 10 and mean is 9. Alexis's median is 8 and mean is 10. If you compare their medians, Romesh is the better player. If you compare their means, Alexis is the better player. In this case, the mean may represent the data better. The median does not consider Alexis's three high scores of 16, 18, and 18. However, these scores help to pull up her mean. Some students may therefore consider Alexis the better player.

---

10. Shannon and Roberto's Social Studies teacher, Mrs. Smith, gives geography quizzes. Here are Shannon's and Roberto's quiz scores.

Shannon	3	9	9	2	9
Roberto	15	4	4	15	3

A. Do you think Shannon would want Mrs. Smith to find her average using the mean or the median? Explain.

B. Do you think Roberto would want Mrs. Smith to find his average using the mean or the median? Explain.

11. During winter break, Romesh and Alexis played a computer game. During the first game, Romesh got to level 5 while Alexis got to level 8. They kept track of how far they got in each game.

Game	Romesh's Level	Alexis's Level
Game 1	5	8
Game 2	10	2
Game 3	7	5
Game 4	3	18
Game 5	11	18
Game 6	14	8
Game 7	12	5
Game 8	10	16

Romesh says he found their averages and decided that he is the better player. Alexis says she found their averages, too. She claims that she is the better player. Can they both be right? Explain.

126   SG • Grade 5 • Unit 4 • Lesson 5   Mean or Median?

Student Guide - page 126

Student Guide (p. 127)

12.* A. Yes, the mean is $63,000.

B. No, most of the employees make between 20–30 thousand dollars. The median would be a better average.

13. A. Median = 47.5 seconds*

B. Mean = 49.2 seconds

---

12. Sometimes, the mean better describes the data. Other times, the median better describes the data. Here are yearly salaries at the Happy Day Manufacturing Company.

Position	Salary
President	$259,000
Vice-President	$123,000
Worker #1	$36,000
Worker #2	$25,000
Worker #3	$18,000
Worker #4	$32,000
Worker #5	$25,000
Worker #6	$22,000
Worker #7	$27,000

The president of the company announced that the average salary was $63,000 a year.

A. Is she correct?

B. Is the mean a good description of the data? Explain.

13. Last summer, Alexis swam the breaststroke in 5 swim meets. Her times are listed below.

56.6 seconds   51.3 seconds   44.8 seconds
       47.5 seconds   45.8 seconds

A. Find her median time.

B. Use a calculator to find the mean.

Mean or Median?   SG • Grade 5 • Unit 4 • Lesson 5   127

Student Guide - page 127

*Answers and/or discussion are included in the Lesson Guide.

14. Ana's group collected data for the lab *Distance vs. Time*. Jerome walked along a track. The rest of the group reported the time he took to walk 6 yards, 9 yards, and 12 yards. Ana was the timer at 6 yards. On the first trial she didn't know how to use the stopwatch. Here is the first row of their data table:

D Distance in Yards	T Time in Seconds			
	Trial 1	Trial 2	Trial 3	Average
6	10	3	5	

A. Find the mean value of the three trials.
B. Find the median value of the three trials.
C. Which average, the median or the mean, represents the data better? Explain your reasoning.

Order of Operations: Using Parentheses

Mr. Moreno showed the class another way to find averages on a calculator. If your calculator has (( ) and ( )) keys, try this method. The (( ) and ( )) are left and right parentheses. Parentheses are often used to show what operations to do first. For example, to find the mean number of points Romesh scored in the first 5 basketball games, we write (4 + 6 + 4 + 23 + 28) ÷ 5. Parentheses say do the work inside the parentheses first.

An example of a **numerical expression** is (4 + 6 + 4 + 23 + 28) ÷ 5. Numerical expressions have numbers and operations. In numerical expressions, we follow the order of operations. That is, we divide and multiply and then add and subtract. When there are parentheses in an expression, we do the calculations inside the parentheses first.

Since we multiply and divide before adding and subtracting,

$$3 \times 2 + 5 = 11 \qquad 6 \div 2 \times 4 + 3 = 15$$
$$3 + 2 \times 5 = 13 \qquad 8 - 6 \div 3 + 4 = 10$$

15. Find the values of the following expressions.
A. 5 + 8 ÷ 4
B. 18 ÷ 3 + 4 × 7
C. 17 − 14 ÷ 2 − 3
D. 6 × 4 ÷ 3 − 2

Student Guide - page 128

Work in parentheses must be done first. For example,

Example A. 3 + 6 ÷ 3 = 5   Example B. 5 × 4 + 2 = 22
(3 + 6) ÷ 3 = 3   5 × (4 + 2) = 30

16. First, find the values of the following expressions without a calculator. Then, use a calculator to check your work.
A. 3 × (12 − 6) =
B. 3 × 12 − 6 =
C. (6 + 3) × (5 − 2) =
D. 6 + 3 × 5 − 2 =
E. 16 ÷ 4 − 2 =
F. 16 ÷ (4 − 2) =
G. 100 ÷ 10 − 5 =
H. 100 ÷ (10 − 5) =

Homework

1. Mr. Moreno's class recorded the daily high and low temperatures in degrees Fahrenheit for 5 days:

Temperature	Monday	Tuesday	Wednesday	Thursday	Friday
High	52°F	38°F	40°F	35°F	48°F
Low	35°F	28°F	30°F	32°F	43°F

A. Find the mean high for the 5 days.
B. Find the mean low for the 5 days.

2. Jessie went bowling with her friends. The first game she bowled 125 points. The second game she bowled 110 points. The third game she bowled 130 points. What was her average score that day? Use the mean.

3. Jessie's team bowled 3 games each. Each team member added their scores for their three games. The totals for the players on her team were 365, 352, 289, and 299. What was the average score for the 4 players on Jessie's team?

4. The heights of 5 players on a basketball team are: 195 cm, 202 cm, 207 cm, 201 cm, and 198 cm.
A. What is the mean height in cm?
B. Estimate the average height in inches. (*Hint:* 100 cm is about 39 in.)
C. Express your answer to Question 4B in feet and inches.

5. Blanca's mother drove a total of 330 miles in 6 hours. What was her mean speed in miles per hour?

Student Guide - page 129

Student Guide (p. 128)

14. A. 6 seconds
   B. 5 seconds*
   C. Median. The first trial involves errors since Ana didn't know how to use the stopwatch. The median is not affected by the extreme value of 10 seconds.*

15. A. 7
   B. 34
   C. 7
   D. 6

Student Guide (p. 129)

16. A. 18   **B.** 30
    C. 27   **D.** 19
    E. 2   **F.** 8
    G. 5   **H.** 20

Homework

1. A. About 43 degrees
   B. About 34 degrees
2. About 122 points
3. About 326 points
4. A. About 200 cm
   B. About 78 inches
   C. About $6\frac{1}{2}$ feet
5. 55 miles per hour

---

*Answers and/or discussion are included in the Lesson Guide.

Student Guide (p. 130)

6. A. 14 years old

   B. 10 years old

   C. The median, since it is not affected by the one extreme value of 48 years old. Most of the students are 11 or under so the mean of 14 years old may not represent the data as well.

7. 12		**8.** 3	
9. 31		**10.** 4	
11. 35		**12.** 5	
13. 47		**14.** 6	
15. 6		**16.** 15	
17. 4		**18.** 27	
19. 2		**20.** 4	
21. 7		**22.** 1	

6. Felicia's piano teacher has 8 students. Each student plays a song in the piano recital. The ages of the students are 7, 48, 10, 10, 11, 11, 6, and 9 years old.

   A. Find the mean age of the students.

   B. Find the median age.

   C. If you can only use one number to represent the ages of the students in the recital, which value would you use—the mean or the median? Explain.

Find the value of the following expressions. Do not use a calculator. Then use a calculator to check your answers.

7. $6 + 3 \times 2 =$

8. $12 \div 2 - 3 =$

9. $7 \times 4 + 3 =$

10. $10 - 2 \times 3 =$

11. $32 + 30 \div 10 =$

12. $5 - 5 \div 5 \times 5 + 5 =$

13. $50 - 9 \div 3 =$

14. $18 - 4 \times 2 \times 6 =$

15. $(50 + 4) \div 9 =$

16. $17 - 20 \div 10 =$

17. $12 \div (6 \div 2) =$

18. $(6 + 3) \times (7 - 4) =$

19. $12 \div (11 - 6 + 1) =$

20. $28 \div (11 - 6 + 2) =$

21. $(17 + 4) \div 3 =$

22. $17 - (64 \div 8) \times 2 =$

130   SG • Grade 5 • Unit 4 • Lesson 5   Mean or Median?

Student Guide - page 130

Lesson 6

Spreading Out

Lesson Overview

In this experiment, students investigate the absorbency of paper towels. They place drops of water on paper towels to explore the relationship between the area of spots relative to the number of drops of water. As students work on this experiment, you have an opportunity to assess their abilities to carry out an investigation and to use data to make predictions and solve problems.

Key Content

- Measuring the area of irregular shapes.
- Collecting, organizing, graphing, and analyzing data.
- Using patterns in data to make predictions and solve problems.
- Drawing and interpreting best-fit lines.
- Choosing an appropriate graph to display data.
- Using ratios to solve problems.
- Averaging: finding the median and mean.

- Using numerical variables.
- Identifying the manipulated, responding, and fixed variables in an experiment.
- Connecting mathematics and science to real-world situations.
- Communicating solutions orally and in writing.

Key Vocabulary

- area
- best-fit line
- fixed variables
- manipulated variable
- responding variable

Math Facts

Assign DPP item S. Review multiplication and division facts for square numbers.

Homework

1. Assign the Homework section in the *Student Guide* after Part 3 of the lab.
2. Assign Part 4 of the Home Practice.

Assessment

1. Use the *Observational Assessment Record* to document students' abilities to measure area and work with data.
2. Use the *TIMS Multidimensional Rubric* to score specific questions from the lab.
3. Use DPP item V as a quiz.
4. Transfer appropriate documentation from the Unit 4 *Observational Assessment Record* to students' *Individual Assessment Record Sheets*.

Curriculum Sequence

Before This Unit

Manipulated and Responding Variables

Students were introduced to the terms manipulated and responding variables as part of the *Bouncing Ball* experiment in Grade 4 Unit 5 Lesson 4. They used the terms throughout the remainder of fourth grade.

Ratios

Students used words, data tables, graphs, and fractions to represent ratios in Unit 3 Lesson 5 *Using Ratios* and in the lab in Lesson 6 *Distance vs. Time.*

After This Unit

Manipulated and Responding Variables

Students identify experimental variables in labs throughout the year.

Ratios

Using ratios to solve problems will be an important topic throughout the remainder of fifth grade. See the following examples: *A Day at the Races* in Unit 5, the study of decimals, percents, and probability in Unit 7, all of Unit 13 *Ratio and Proportion, Circumference vs. Diameter* in Unit 14, and *Bats* in Unit 16.

Materials List

Supplies and Copies

Student	Teacher
Supplies for Each Student • calculator • ruler **Supplies for Each Student Group** • 1–2 pairs of scissors • eyedropper • 3–4 sheets of the same brand of paper towel • small container of water • 2 books or 1 geoboard (for drying the paper towels)	**Supplies**
Copies • 1 copy of *Centimeter Grid Paper* per student or more as needed (*Unit Resource Guide* Page 44) • 1 copy of *Three-trial Data Table* per student or more as needed (*Unit Resource Guide* Page 129) • 2 copies of *Centimeter Graph Paper* per student (*Unit Resource Guide* Page 130)	**Copies/Transparencies** • 1 transparency of *Centimeter Graph Paper*, optional (*Unit Resource Guide* Page 130) • 1 transparency of *Bar Graph or Point Graph?*, optional (*Unit Resource Guide* Page 127) • 1 transparency of *Spot Check*, optional (*Unit Resource Guide* Page 128)

All blackline masters including assessment, transparency, and DPP masters are also on the Teacher Resource CD.

Student Books

Spreading Out (*Student Guide* Pages 131–138)
Student Rubric: *Telling* (*Student Guide* Appendix C and Inside Back Cover), optional

Daily Practice and Problems and Home Practice

DPP items S–X (*Unit Resource Guide* Pages 27–29)
Home Practice Part 4 (*Discovery Assignment Book* Page 45)

Note: Classrooms whose pacing differs significantly from the suggested pacing of the units should use the Math Facts Calendar in Section 4 of the *Facts Resource Guide* to ensure students receive the complete math facts program.

Assessment Tools

Observational Assessment Record (*Unit Resource Guide* Pages 13–14)
Individual Assessment Record Sheet (*Teacher Implementation Guide,* Assessment section)

Daily Practice and Problems

Suggestions for using the DPPs are on pages 122–124.

S. Bit: Multiplying and Dividing
by Multiples of 10 (URG p. 27)

A. $800 \times 80 =$ B. $25,000 \div 50 =$
C. $4900 \div 7 =$ D. $10,000 \div 10 =$
E. $40 \times 400 =$ F. $8100 \div 90 =$

T. Challenge: Within 10%?
(URG p. 27)

Jerome, Lin, Nicholas, and Alexis each estimate the number of marshmallows in a jar. Jerome's estimate is 131. Lin's estimate is 120. Nicholas's estimate is 100. Alexis estimates there are 135 marshmallows in the jar. The jar actually contains 111 marshmallows. Which estimates are within 10% of 111? How do you know?

U. Bit: More Shortcut Division
(URG p. 27)

Use a paper-and-pencil method to solve the following problems. Estimate to make sure your answers are reasonable.

A. $3315 \div 6 =$
B. $927 \div 7 =$
C. $3476 \div 4 =$

V. Task: Ratios (URG p. 28)

Manny put 1, 2, and 4 drops of liquid on three pieces of the same brand of paper towel. He counted the area of each spot formed. His data are shown below.

N Number of Drops	A Area (sq cm)
1	7
2	15
4	28

1. Graph Manny's data on a piece of *Centimeter Graph Paper.* Graph the number of drops on the horizontal axis and the area on the vertical axis.

2. If Manny put 6 drops of liquid on the paper towel, predict the approximate area of the new spot.

3. Write three equal ratios, in the form of a fraction, for the ratio of the area to the number of drops. Use ratios from your graph.

W. Bit: Decorating the House
(URG p. 29)

Jackie wants to cut rectangles from material to make rugs for her miniature doll house. She measures the living room and family room floors. Her measurements are listed below. Find the area of the floor in each of these rooms.

Living room: 7 cm by 9 cm

Family room: 7 cm by 11 cm

X. Challenge: What's That
Number? (URG p. 29)

Find a number between 200 and 300 that is divisible by 2, 3, and 5. What strategies did you use?

Spreading Out

Mr. Moreno spilled a cup of coffee on his desk. Arti and Jessie ran to get some paper towels to clean up the coffee.

"Don't grab those school towels!" said Arti. "They don't absorb much."

"I'll get the paper towels from over the sink," said Jessie.

"Thanks," said Mr. Moreno. "I was afraid that coffee would run everywhere."

"How much liquid can a paper towel absorb?" asked Jessie.

"We can always test the paper towels to find out," said Arti.

"That's a great idea for an experiment," said Mr. Moreno. "We can test each towel by dropping a few drops of water from an eyedropper onto it."

Spreading Out — SG • Grade 5 • Unit 4 • Lesson 6 **131**

Student Guide - page 131

Before the Lab

The extended list of concepts in the Key Content section at the beginning of the Lesson Guide shows that this lab provides a context for many math and science concepts. Students had some experience with most of these concepts in preceding grades and units. However, in this lab we ask students to apply the concepts in new ways. For example, although they used means and medians to average data in fourth grade, in this lab they must also consider which average (mean or median) best represents their data. As you read the Lesson Guide and prepare to teach the lab, consider your students' needs. For students new to the curriculum, you may decide to emphasize some concepts more than others, provide more guidance for some parts of the lab, or delete some questions. For example, students who did not complete optional Lesson 4 should not be assigned the problems using 10% as a standard for error in measurements. On the other hand, for students who have had experience with most of these concepts, this lab can challenge them to apply these important ideas in a real-world situation. Discussion prompts in the Lesson Guide and questions in the *Student Guide* are designed to help students make connections between the concepts.

Teaching the Lab

Part 1 Defining the Variables and Drawing the Picture

The first few *Spreading Out* Lab Pages in the *Student Guide* set the stage for this activity. Read these pages as a class or ask students to read the pages in small groups. The Identifying Variables section uses the terms "manipulated" and "responding variable" for the first time in fifth grade. (See the TIMS Tutor: *The TIMS Laboratory Method* for more information on variables in experiments.) Identify these two main variables in the lab. The number *(N)* of drops used is the **manipulated variable,** since Arti and Jessie chose the values for the number of drops before they began collecting data. The area *(A)* of the spots is the **responding variable** since they find the values for area by doing the experiment. Expand on this discussion of variables using the following prompts:

* *Think about the experiments we have done this year. For example, think about the lab* Distance vs. Time. *What are the two main variables in that lab?* (Distance and time)

* *Which variable had values we chose before we started collecting data?* (Distance. The three distances that were timed were measured out and written in the data table before data collection.)

Student Guide - page 132

"I think we should try three different numbers of drops so we have enough data to look for patterns," said Jessie. "We should start with numbers (of drops) that have a pattern. Then it will be easier to see how changing the number of drops changes the area of the spots. We should also do three trials as we did in *Distance vs. Time*. Then, if the areas of the spots for all three trials are close, we will know we didn't make any big mistakes."

Identifying Variables
"As you were talking, you identified the two main variables in your experiment," said Mr. Moreno. "The variables are number of drops (N) and area (A). The two main variables in an experiment have special names. The variable with values we know in the beginning of the experiment is called the **manipulated variable**. We often choose the values of the manipulated variable before collecting the data."

Arti and Jessie chose 1 drop, 2 drops, and 4 drops as the values for the number of drops, so that the spots they made would not be too big. They made three spots of water with 1 drop, three spots of water with 2 drops, and three spots with 4 drops of water on paper towels.

"The variable with values obtained by doing the experiment is called the **responding variable**," said Mr. Moreno. "Your responding variable is the area of the spots. The area of each spot changes, depending upon the number of drops of water you use."

Mr. Moreno added, "There are other variables that can affect the size of the spots. For example, if we use a bigger eyedropper or a different liquid, the size of the spots might be different. These other variables should stay the same during the whole experiment. In this way, the only thing that affects the area of the spots is the number of drops. The other variables that stay the same are called **fixed variables**."

When the spots had dried a little, Arti and Jessie traced around each spot with a pencil. They used scissors to cut out each spot. They then measured the area of each spot and recorded it in a data table.

Student Guide - page 133

- *Which variable is the manipulated variable?* (Distance)
- *For which variable did we find values by doing the experiment?* (Time. Students recorded the time in their data tables after the walker finished walking.)
- *Which variable is the responding variable?* (Time)
- *Think about the experiment* Searching the Forest. *What are the two main variables?* (Color and Number)
- *Which variable was the manipulated variable? That is, for which variable did you know the values before you collected data?* (Color. Students knew the possible colors of tiles before they drew their samples from the bag.)
- *Which variable is the responding variable? That is, for which variable did you find the values by collecting the data?* (Number. They counted and recorded the number of each color as part of the data collection.)

Bar Graph or Point Graph?
Arti and Jessie decided to graph their data. They wanted to see if there were any patterns that could help them find the number of drops of water the paper towel can absorb.

"I think we should make a bar graph," said Arti.

"I think we should make a point graph," said Jessie. "Which kind of graph is best?"

"Let's do both kinds of graphs and find out," said Arti.

Arti made a bar graph, and Jessie made a point graph as shown.

"You were right, Jessie," said Arti. "The point graph is better. We can find the area for any number of drops by using the line. See, I can find the area of a spot with 6 drops like this."

"There are times when it is good to make a bar graph and times when it is good to make a point graph," said Mr. Moreno. "We make a point graph when both variables are numerical and when it makes sense to think about values between the data points. For example, it makes sense to think about the area of a spot made with 3 drops of water. This information lies between the data for 2 drops and 4 drops. By fitting a line to the points, we can find the area of a spot made with 3 drops. We can also find the area of a spot made with 6 drops."

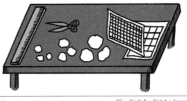

Student Guide - page 134

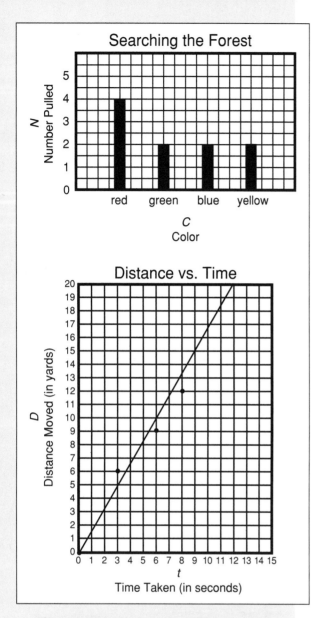

Figure 17: *Examples of bar and point graphs*

The Bar Graph or Point Graph? section of the *Spreading Out* Activity Pages in the *Student Guide* discusses choosing the appropriate type of graph based on the variables in the lab. You can connect these concepts to labs in previous units using the *Bar Graph or Point Graph?* Transparency Master and these prompts:

- *Look at the two graphs on the overhead. We used a bar graph for the* Searching the Forest *graph. Does it make sense to talk about data points in between the colors?* (Since color is a categorical variable, it doesn't make sense to talk about values between green and blue.)

- *Why did we use a point graph for the* Distance vs. Time *graph?* (It makes sense to talk about values for time between 3 seconds and 6 seconds and we wanted to use the graph to make predictions about values beyond the data points.)

Use **Questions 1–4** in the *Student Guide* to check students' understanding of the experiment. **Question 1** asks how to measure the area of the spots. One way is to outline the spots with a pencil after the water stops spreading. When the spots are dry enough, students cut them out and trace them on *Centimeter Grid Paper.* Once the spots are traced on the grid paper, students should label them with the number of drops used to make the spot. Lesson 1 *Grid Area* reviewed the technique for finding the area of the spots shown in Figure 18.

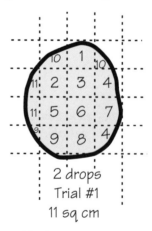

Figure 18: *Counting the area of a spot*

Students identify the manipulated and responding variables in *Question 2.* To look for the relationship between these two variables (the number of drops and the area of the spot), other variables in the experiment must be kept **fixed** *(Question 3).* These include:

1. Type of paper towel.
2. Type of liquid. (Water is used throughout the experiment.)
3. The size of the drop. (To ensure drops of the same size, it is best to use the same eyedropper for all drops.)
4. Procedure for making spots. (Drop each drop in the center of the spot you are making. Keep the eyedropper at the same level above the towel for each drop.)

Students should keep the towel off the desk's surface until their spot has dried enough to cut it out. One way to do this is to place the paper towel on the top of a geoboard. Another way is to place two books on the desk a little closer together than the width of the paper towel. The edges of the paper towel are placed between the pages of each book so it is lifted above the desk's surface, as in Figure 19.

Figure 19: *Two methods for keeping the paper towel off the desk top*

Question 4 asks why it is a good idea to conduct more than one trial. A quick response from students is, "We might make a mistake." In the experiment, error can occur in several ways. First, counting square centimeters does not allow us to find the area exactly. Second, it is not always possible to keep all the fixed variables constant. For instance, using the same eyedropper may not ensure the same size drops since students often have trouble controlling the bulb of the eyedropper when making spots. Scientists use multiple trials to average out the error that is inevitable in an experiment and to check for large errors. (*Questions 6C and 6E* discuss ways to check for large errors.)

Discuss

1. Describe how Arti and Jessie can measure the area of the spots they made.
2. A. What are the two main variables in the lab?
   B. Which variable is the manipulated variable?
   C. Which variable is the responding variable?
3. What variables should be held fixed so that Arti and Jessie can see how changing the number of drops affects the area of the spots?
4. Why is it a good idea to make more than one trial?

Draw

5. Design a lab to find out what happens to the area if you change the number of drops of water used to make the spot. Draw a picture of your plan.
   A. Label the variables in your picture.
   B. Choose values for the number of drops. (You may choose 1, 2, and 4 drops as Arti and Jessie did, or you may choose other values.)

Collect

6. Work with your partner(s) to collect data and record it in a table. Discuss the following before you begin:
   A. How many trials will you need to make? That is, how many times will you make a spot for each number of drops?
   B. How will you organize your data in a data table?
   C. How can you check for mistakes in dropping the water to make the spots?
   D. What unit of measure will you use when finding the area?
   E. How will you check to be sure your data is reasonable?
7. Look at the data you have collected. Will you use the mean or median value to average the data?

Student Guide - page 135 (Answers on p. 131)

After the discussion, students begin the experiment using *Questions 5–9* on the *Spreading Out* Lab Pages in the *Student Guide.* They draw a picture of the experimental setup and label the main variables *(Question 5A).* The picture allows you to see if students have a clear understanding of the method and variables and are ready to proceed.

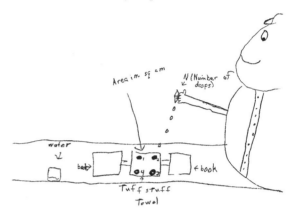

Figure 20: *Sample student drawing*

As part of designing their experiments, students choose values for the number of drops. *(Question 5B)* Discuss the values that Jessie and Arti chose and decide as a class if these are the ones you will also use. Students should choose values that are manageable and show a pattern for the relationship of area to the number of drops. Note that *Questions 10–11* ask students to interpolate and extrapolate for 3 and 5 drops from their data. Students should not use these numbers of drops in their experiment.

Part 2 **Collecting Data**

Question 6 asks students to make decisions concerning the collecting and recording of the data. *Questions 6A–6B* ask them to decide how many trials they will make and how they will organize their data. You can provide further structure for students by giving them a copy of a blank *Three-trial Data Table.* Figure 21 shows sample data for the experiment.

Spreading Out

N Number of Drops	A Area (in sq cm)			
	Trial 1	Trial 2	Trial 3	Average
1	$5\frac{1}{2}$	4	$6\frac{1}{2}$	5
2	17	15	14	15
4	26	30	27	28

Figure 21: *Sample* Three-trial Data Table *using the mean (rounded to the nearest whole centimeter)*

Question 6C asks students how they can check for mistakes in dropping the water to make spots. Remind students that they should make their spots so each is clearly defined and they do not run together. Use the *Spot Check* Transparency Master to encourage students to check for obvious errors in making spots before they count square centimeters. The transparency shows three spots made by a fifth-grade student for one, two, and four drops of water. Ask:

- *Are the spots for each number of drops all about the same size? What should the experimenter do?* (No, one of the spots for one drop is much larger than the other spots for one drop. The experimenter should try to make another spot with one drop so all three drops are about the same size. Since one of the spots for two drops is much smaller than the other spots for two drops, the experimenter should again try to make spots of about the same size with two drops. The spots for four drops are about the same size, so the experimenter can measure the area of these spots by counting square centimeters.)

Students count square centimeters to measure the area of each spot *(Question 6D)* and record each area in their data tables. Then before they graph the data, they should check to see if their data are reasonable. No single measurement should be much bigger or smaller than the others. If students completed optional Lesson 4 *How Close Is Close Enough?,* they can use 10% as a standard for error among their measurements *(Question 6E).*

Observe students working and recording data. Are they carefully using the eyedroppers? Do the groups look over their measurements to see if they are reasonable? If they find data points that are not reasonable, encourage them to find reasons for the differences. Did the spots run together? Did they have trouble controlling the number of drops? Help them make informed decisions about how to handle the data.

Question 7 asks students to decide whether to use the mean or the median to average the data. The data in the table in Figure 21 shows the mean values rounded to the nearest whole centimeter. Since the mean and the median for this data are nearly the same, either average can be used to represent the data. If students use the mean, encourage them to use their calculators and to round to the nearest whole centimeter.

Content Note

Using 10% as a standard is not intended to involve lengthy arithmetic procedures nor to be used as a rigid rule. (See Lesson 4.) Instead, students should develop the number sense needed for rough mental calculations and estimates. For example, they should recognize that 10% of any measurement less than 10 sq cm is less than 1 sq cm. So, the areas made with 1 drop of water ($5\frac{1}{2}$ sq cm, 4 sq cm, and $6\frac{1}{2}$ sq cm) recorded in Figure 21 are not within 1 sq cm of one another, nor is 4 sq cm within 1 sq cm of the median value of $5\frac{1}{2}$ sq cm. These data do not strictly fall within our 10% limits. However, given the difficulty of controlling the variables, students can use this data.

If students did not complete Lesson 4, they do not need to use the 10% standard. However, they should check to see that their measurements are reasonable.

N Number of Drops	A Area (in sq cm)			
	Trial 1	Trial 2	Trial 3	Average
1	17	8	6	8
2	15	7	12	12
4	27	23	19	23

Figure 22: *Sample data table for* Spreading Out *using the median*

TIMS Tip

Have students save their paper towels. They will need them to answer **Question 11.**

8. Make a graph of your data on a sheet of graph paper.
   • Graph the number of drops (N) on the horizontal axis and the area (A) on the vertical axis.
   • The vertical axis should be numbered to at least 40 sq cm.
   • What is the area of a spot made with zero drops? Add this point to your graph.

9. If the points on your graph suggest a line, use a ruler to draw a best-fit line.

Write the answers to these questions. Use your graph and your data table to help you.

10. **A.** Use your graph to predict the area of a spot made with three drops of water. Show your work on your graph, and record your prediction.
    B. Make a spot using three drops of water. Find the area.
    C. Was your prediction within 10% of the actual area? Explain why or why not.

11. **A.** Use your graph to predict the area of a spot made with five drops of water. Show your work on your graph, and record your prediction.
    B. Check your prediction by making a spot with five drops. Find the area of the spot.
    C. Was your prediction within 10% of the actual area? Explain why or why not.

12. **A.** If you want to make a spot with an area of 40 sq cm, how many drops should you use? Explain how you solved this problem.
    B. Find another way to solve this problem. Explain.

136   SG • Grade 5 • Unit 4 • Lesson 6   Spreading Out

Student Guide - page 136 (Answers on p. 131)

If the range between the data points is large as in the data in the table in Figure 22, students may need to make other choices. For example, of the three measurements for the area of spots with 1 drop, 17 sq cm is more than twice either of the other two measurements. Similarly, the data for spots made with 2 drops include a data point that is a little more than half of the other two.

In cases like this, students will need to make informed decisions about using their data. The preferred option is to conduct more trials. However, it may not be practical to get out the equipment and collect more data. Students can also choose to throw out the data points that are significantly different from the others and average the remaining two measurements. As a third option, students can choose to use the median to represent the data instead of the mean, since the median is not as affected by extreme values. Figure 22 shows the medians for the data in the table.

Part 3   Graphing the Data

Question 8 asks students to graph the data. Remind students to make a point graph of the data. Discuss the reasons for using points instead of bars. Each student adds a point at (0 drops, 0 sq cm) to the graph since zero drops will produce a spot with zero area. Then he or she uses a ruler to fit a line to all four points on the graph **(Question 9).** A sample student graph of the data in Figure 21 is shown in Figure 23.

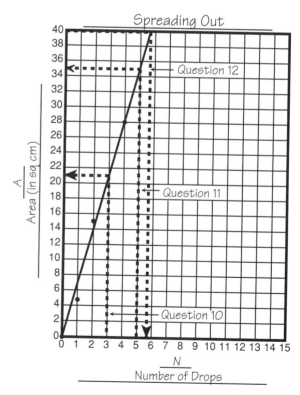

Figure 23: *Sample student graph*

Use *Questions 10–14* to explore the results of the experiment. *Questions 10–11* provide opportunities for students to use their graphs and data tables to solve problems. Using their best-fit lines, students predict the area of spots made with three drops and five drops of water. For example, using the best-fit line on the sample graph, a reasonable prediction for the area of a spot made with three drops is 21 sq cm. Notice how this is shown on the graph. Students can check their predictions by making spots with three drops of water and counting the areas. If students find their predictions are not close, they can go back and look for errors in dropping water to make spots, counting square centimeters, and drawing a best-fit line.

Question 12 asks students to find the number of drops needed to make a spot with an area of 40 sq cm using two different strategies. This problem can be solved using a graph if the vertical axis is scaled to include 40 sq cm. (See Figure 23.) Using data from the graph, about 6 drops will make a spot with an area of about 40 sq cm. Students can check their predictions by making spots with 6 drops of water and finding the areas. Other strategies are possible. For example, if a three-drop spot makes a spot with an area of 21 sq cm, then a 6-drop spot will have an area of a little more than 40 sq cm.

To answer *Question 13,* students must combine their knowledge of area, ratios, and graphs. To answer *Question 13A,* a student must select a point on his or her best-fit line and use it to write the ratio *(A/N)* of the area of a spot to the number of drops. Encourage students to use points where the line crosses grid lines. Using the graph in Figure 23, we can write $A/N = 14$ sq cm/2 drops. *Question 13B* asks students to estimate the area covered by 12 drops. Students can use equivalent fractions to solve the problem:

$$\frac{14 \text{ sq cm}}{2 \text{ drops}} = \frac{14 \times 6}{2 \times 6} = \frac{84 \text{ sq cm}}{12 \text{ drops}}$$

Solutions will vary based on differences in data. Other strategies are also possible. Encourage students to discuss their answers and give reasons for the differences.

To answer *Question 13C,* students find the area of one sheet of the paper towels they used during the experiment and then estimate the number of drops the paper towel will absorb. If the dimensions of a paper towel are 28 cm by 23 cm, the area of the paper towel is 644 sq cm. Using the sample data from Figure 23, two drops cover an area of 14 sq cm. So, using a

---

13. **A.** Choose a point on your line. Use it to write the ratio of the area of a spot to the number of drops as a fraction $(\frac{A}{N})$.

   B. Estimate the area covered by 12 drops of water.

   C. Estimate the number of drops of water one sheet of your paper towel will absorb. Explain how you solved this problem. Use the Student Rubric: *Telling* to help you write about your solution.

14. Jessie and Arti used Super Soak paper towels in their experiment. Jerome and Lee Yah used Absorb-Plus paper towels. Their graphs are shown here. Which paper towel can hold more water?

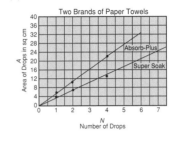

Spreading Out   SG • Grade 5 • Unit 4 • Lesson 6   **137**

Student Guide - page 137 (Answers on p. 132)

TIMS Tip

If your students did not complete Lesson 4 of this unit, *How Close Is Close Enough?,* skip questions that suggest the use of 10% as an indicator of accuracy in measurement. Skip *Questions 10C and 11C.*

If students completed Lesson 4, they can decide if their predictions are reasonable by determining if they are within 10 percent of their counted areas. For example, a student makes a three-drop spot and finds that the area is 26 sq cm. He or she estimates that 10% of 26 is between 2 and 3 sq cm and reasons that 21 sq cm is not within the acceptable range.

TIMS Tip

You can use *Question 13* to assess students' abilities to solve problems using data and communicate their solutions. Explain to students your expectations of their responses by reviewing the Student Rubric: *Telling* before they begin writing up their solutions.

Homework

You will need a sheet of graph paper and a ruler to complete this homework.

1. Professor Peabody tested Whizzo brand paper towels. He noticed a very interesting pattern in his data. Then, his pet mouse, Milo, tracked ink across his data table. Look for a pattern in Professor Peabody's data.

N Number of Drops	*A* Area of Spot in sq cm
1	
2	
	8
8	16

A. Copy the data table on your paper and fill in the missing values.
B. Make a point graph of the data. Graph the number of drops on the horizontal axis and the area on the vertical axis. Use a ruler to fit a line to the points.
C. What would be the area of a spot made with no drops? Add this point to your graph.

2. A. Choose a point on the graph. Use it to write the ratio ($\frac{A}{N}$) of the area to the number of drops.
   B. Using fractions, write two ratios equal to the ratio in Question 2A.
3. A. What area would 6 drops make on a Whizzo brand paper towel?
   B. How many drops are needed to make a spot with an area of 28 sq cm? Show your work.

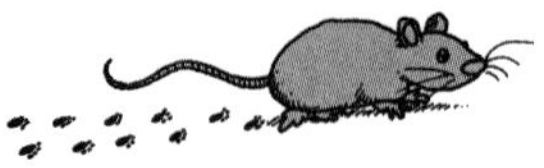

138 SG • Grade 5 • Unit 4 • Lesson 6 Spreading Out

***Student Guide* - page 138** *(Answers on p. 132)*

Name ______________________ Date ______________

PART 4 Comparing Prices

While stocking shelves at her father's store, Arti compares the prices of two different brands of pencils. She showed the information in the following graphs. Use the graphs to answer the questions below. Use a separate sheet of paper for your explanations.

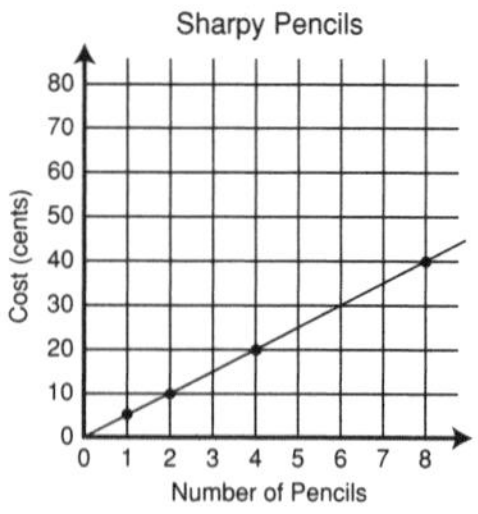

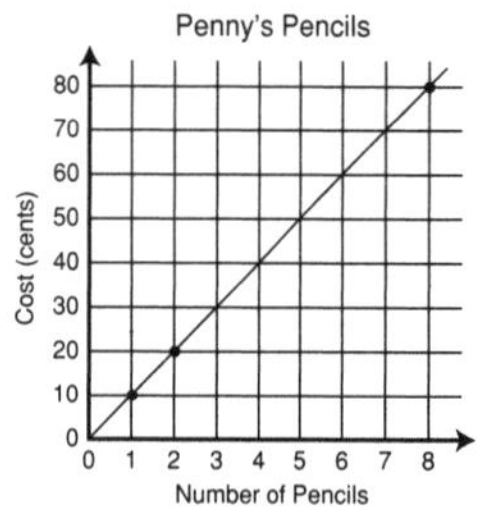

1. Write a ratio of cost to the number of pencils for Sharpy Pencils.
2. Write a ratio of cost to number of pencils for Penny's Pencils.
3. Which pencils are more expensive? How do you know?
4. Which line is steeper?

Show as many ways as you can to solve the following problems.

5. What is the cost of four Sharpy Pencils?
6. How many of Penny's Pencils can you buy with 60¢?
7. How many Sharpy Pencils can you buy with 60¢?

DIVISION AND DATA DAB • Grade 5 • Unit 4 45

***Discovery Assignment Book* - page 45** *(Answers on p. 133)*

calculator (644 sq cm ÷ 14 sq cm = 46 spots) we find that the paper towel would be covered by about 46 two-spot drops. So, the paper towel can absorb about 2 × 46 or about 90–100 drops. Student groups are likely to develop several alternative strategies for solving this problem.

Students must analyze the graph in Figure 24 to answer ***Question 14.*** Students should conclude that *Super Soak* paper towels are the most absorbent because each drop covers less area, so the towel can soak up more drops in a smaller area.

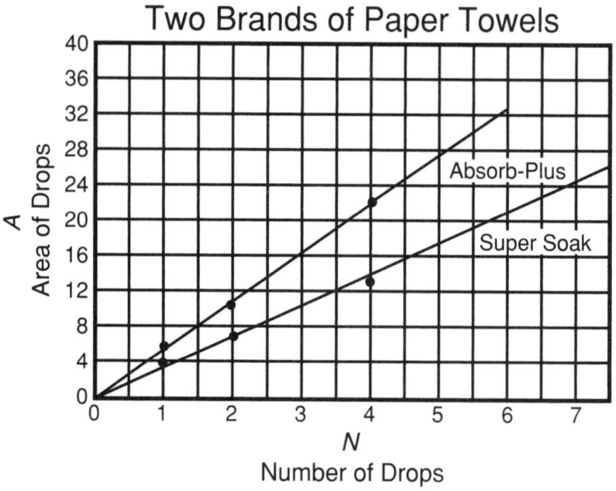

Figure 24: *Lines for different brands of paper towels*

Math Facts

DPP item S provides practice with multiplication and division with multiples of ten.

Homework and Practice

- The Homework section of the *Student Guide* and DPP item V provide practice plotting points and writing ratios. If you assign these before students solve ***Question 13*** in the Explore section, they will have practiced the skills needed in ***Question 13.***
- DPP Bit U provides in-class practice with paper-and-pencil division. DPP Bit W provides practice finding area.
- Assign Part 4 of the Home Practice, which involves reading and interpreting graphs.

Answers for Part 4 of the Home Practice are in the Answer Key at the end of this lesson and at the end of this unit.

- Use the *Observational Assessment Record* in the *Unit Resource Guide* to record student success in measuring area, making an appropriate graph, and working with data.

- Use one or more dimensions of the *TIMS Multidimensional Rubric* to score student responses to **Question 13** in the Explore section of the *Student Guide.* Encourage students to use the Student Rubric: *Telling* to guide them as they describe their solution strategies. You can also encourage them to use the Student Rubrics: *Knowing* and *Solving.* Tell students your expectations before they work on the problem. If a student has trouble getting started, such as needing help finding the area of a paper towel, record this information and include it in your evaluation. After students solve the problem and write a draft, give them suggestions for improving their work. You may ask a student to correct some calculations, include all the steps in the process, display the data in an organized manner, or check the solution using another method. Score their revisions and add them to their collection folders for possible inclusion in their portfolios.

- To grade the lab, teachers often assign points to one or more sections of the lab. See the Evaluating Labs section of the *Assessment* section in the *Teacher Implementation Guide* for specific suggestions for grading all sections of the lab. If you choose to grade only one section, grading the picture is appropriate since identifying the manipulated and responding variables and keeping all other variables held fixed are important features of the lab. You can use the following criteria:

- Is the variable number of drops *(N)* clearly represented and labeled?

- Is the variable area of the spots *(A)* clearly represented and labeled?

- Are the procedure and materials illustrated? Can another person look at the picture and do the experiment? For example, does the student show how the paper towel was raised off the desk. See Figure 20 for an example. Note that this student drew a beaker of water to represent that the type of liquid is held fixed and gave the brand name of the paper towel to show that the type of towel is also held fixed.

- Use DPP item V as a quiz on ratios and drawing and interpreting best-fit lines.

- Transfer appropriate documentation from the Unit 4 *Observational Assessment Record* to students' *Individual Assessment Record Sheets.*

Extension

- Purchase two or more brands of paper towels. Give half the class one brand and the other half the second brand. Give each group 3–4 sheets of the same brand. Repeat the experiment. Compare differences in the data. Find the most absorbent and the least absorbent paper towel.

- Assign DPP Challenges T and X. Use item T only if students completed Lesson 4.

Software Connection

Use a graphing program, such as *Graph Master,* to graph and help analyze the data. If you use *Graph Master,* the manipulated variable in the experiment (number of drops in *Spreading Out*) is the independent variable and the responding variable (area of the spots in *Spreading Out*) is the dependent variable. Using a graphing utility allows students to easily modify components of the graph, such as the scales on the horizontal and vertical axes.

Estimated Class Sessions 3-4

At a Glance

Math Facts and Daily Practice and Problems
Assign DPP items S–X. Review multiplication and division facts for square numbers.

Part 1. Defining the Variables and Drawing the Picture
1. Read the first few *Spreading Out* Lab Pages in the *Student Guide* to introduce the lab.
2. Use the Identifying the Variables section of the *Student Guide* to name the two main variables in the lab (the manipulated and responding variables) and the variables that must be held fixed.
3. Use the *Bar Graph or Point Graph?* Transparency Master and the discussion prompts in the Lesson Guide to help students choose the appropriate type of graph.
4. Discuss *Questions 1–4.*
5. Students draw pictures of their experiments. *(Question 5)*

Part 2. Collecting Data
1. Remind students of the procedures for collecting the data.
2. Students decide on the number of spots to use, the number of trials, how to check if their data are reasonable, and how to organize the data tables. *(Question 6)*
3. Students collect and record their data in their data tables.
4. Students decide whether to use the mean or the median. *(Question 7)*

Part 3. Graphing the Data
1. Students plot their data and add (0 drops, 0 sq cm) to their graphs. *(Question 8)*
2. Students use a ruler to draw the best-fit line. *(Question 9)*

Part 4. Exploring the Data
1. Students make predictions and check them. *(Questions 10–12)*
2. Use *Question 13* to assess students' abilities to solve an open-ended problem and communicate solution strategies.
3. Students discuss their responses to the questions.
4. Students add the labs and their solution to *Question 13* to their collection folders.

Homework
1. Assign the Homework section in the *Student Guide* after Part 3 of the lab.
2. Assign Part 4 of the Home Practice.

Assessment
1. Use the *Observational Assessment Record* to document students' abilities to measure area and work with data.
2. Use the *TIMS Multidimensional Rubric* to score specific questions from the lab.
3. Use DPP item V as a quiz.
4. Transfer appropriate documentation from the Unit 4 *Observational Assessment Record* to students' *Individual Assessment Record Sheets.*

URG • Grade 5 • Unit 4 • Lesson 6   125

At a Glance

Extension

1. Repeat the experiment by comparing two different brands of towels.
2. Assign DPP Challenges T and X.

Connection

Use a graphing program such as *Graph Master* to graph and analyze the data.

Answer Key is on pages 131–133.

Notes:

Bar Graph or Point Graph?

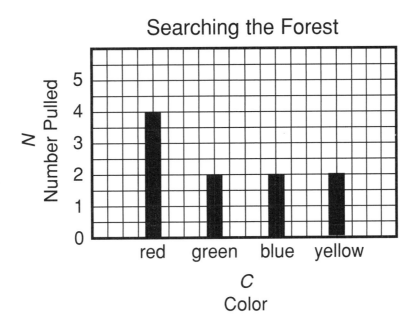

Searching the Forest

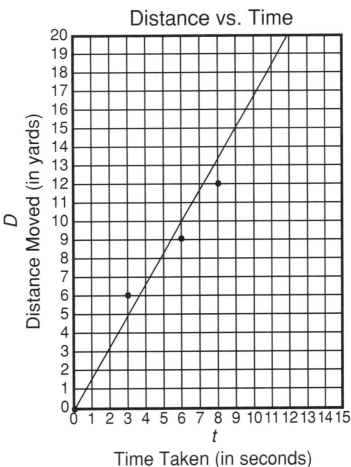

Distance vs. Time

Spot Check

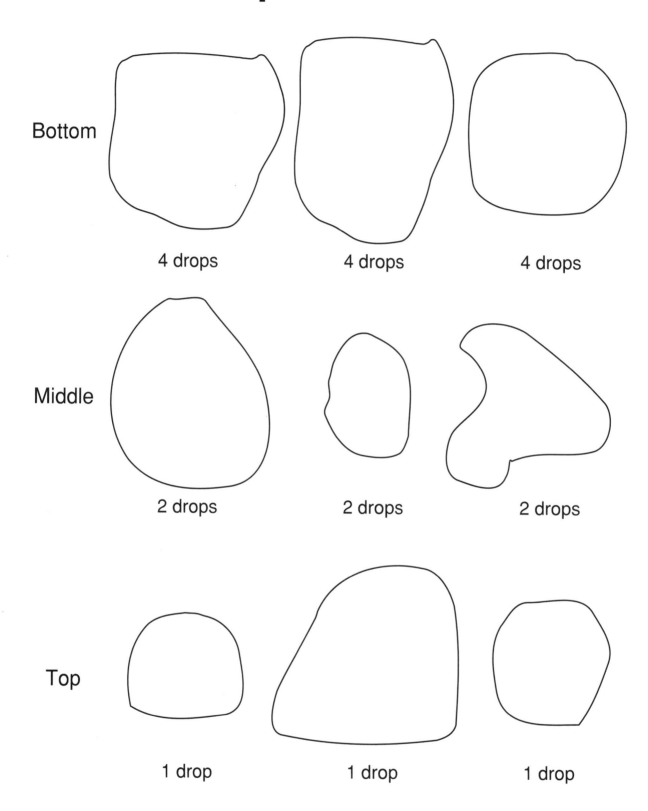

Bottom

4 drops   4 drops   4 drops

Middle

2 drops   2 drops   2 drops

Top

1 drop   1 drop   1 drop

Transparency Master

_____

	Trial 1	Trial 2	Trial 3	Average

Name _____   Date _____

Centimeter Graph Paper, Blackline Master

Student Guide (p. 135)

1. Arti and Jessie can trace their spot onto *Centimeter Grid Paper* and count out the whole and partial square centimeters to find the area.*

2.* **A.** Number of Drops and Area

   B. Number of Drops

   C. Area

3. Students each time should use the same type of paper towel, the same liquid, and the same eyedropper. They should drop each drop into the center of the spot, keep the eyedropper at the same level when they drop, and keep the paper towel off the desk.*

4. Making more than one trial helps to eliminate experimental error.*

5. **A.** A sample picture is shown in Figure 20 in Lesson Guide 6.*

   B. Answers will vary.

6.* **A.–E.** Two sample data tables are shown in Figures 21 and 22 in Lesson Guide 6.

7. Students should use the average that is most appropriate for their data.

Discuss

1. Describe how Arti and Jessie can measure the area of the spots they made.
2. **A.** What are the two main variables in the lab?
   B. Which variable is the manipulated variable?
   C. Which variable is the responding variable?
3. What variables should be held fixed so that Arti and Jessie can see how changing the number of drops affects the area of the spots?
4. Why is it a good idea to make more than one trial?

Draw

5. Design a lab to find out what happens to the area if you change the number of drops of water used to make the spot. Draw a picture of your plan.
   A. Label the variables in your picture.
   B. Choose values for the number of drops. (You may choose 1, 2, and 4 drops as Arti and Jessie did, or you may choose other values.)

Collect

6. Work with your partner(s) to collect data and record it in a table. Discuss the following before you begin:
   A. How many trials will you need to make? That is, how many times will you make a spot for each number of drops?
   B. How will you organize your data in a data table?
   C. How can you check for mistakes in dropping the water to make the spots?
   D. What unit of measure will you use when finding the area?
   E. How will you check to be sure your data is reasonable?
7. Look at the data you have collected. Will you use the mean or median value to average the data?

Spreading Out   SG • Grade 5 • Unit 4 • Lesson 6   **135**

Student Guide - page 135

Student Guide (p. 136)

8.–9. A sample graph is shown in Figure 23 in Lesson Guide 6. Zero drops makes zero area. The point (0 drops, 0 sq cm) is added to the sample graph in Figure 23 in Lesson Guide 6.*

10.* **A.** Using sample graph in Figure 23, 21 sq cm.

   B.–C. Answers will vary.

11.* **A.** Using sample graph in Figure 23, 35 sq cm.

   B.–C. Answers will vary.

12.* **A.** Using sample graph in Figure 23, about 6 drops.

   B. Strategies will vary. Students could use ratios.

Graph

8. Make a graph of your data on a sheet of graph paper.
   • Graph the number of drops (*N*) on the horizontal axis and the area (*A*) on the vertical axis.
   • The vertical axis should be numbered to at least 40 sq cm.
   • What is the area of a spot made with zero drops? Add this point to your graph.
9. If the points on your graph suggest a line, use a ruler to draw a best-fit line.

Explore

Write the answers to these questions. Use your graph and your data table to help you.

10. **A.** Use your graph to predict the area of a spot made with three drops of water. Show your work on your graph, and record your prediction.
    B. Make a spot using three drops of water. Find the area.
    C. Was your prediction within 10% of the actual area? Explain why or why not.
11. **A.** Use your graph to predict the area of a spot made with five drops of water. Show your work on your graph, and record your prediction.
    B. Check your prediction by making a spot with five drops. Find the area of the spot.
    C. Was your prediction within 10% of the actual area? Explain why or why not.
12. **A.** If you want to make a spot with an area of 40 sq cm, how many drops should you use? Explain how you solved this problem.
    B. Find another way to solve this problem. Explain.

136   SG • Grade 5 • Unit 4 • Lesson 6   Spreading Out

Student Guide - page 136

*Answers and/or discussion are included in the Lesson Guide.

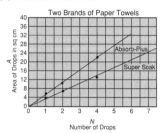

13. A. Choose a point on your line. Use it to write the ratio of the area of a spot to the number of drops as a fraction ($\frac{A}{N}$).

B. Estimate the area covered by 12 drops of water.

C. Estimate the number of drops of water one sheet of your paper towel will absorb. Explain how you solved this problem. Use the Student Rubric: *Telling* to help you write about your solution.

14. Jessie and Arti used Super Soak paper towels in their experiment. Jerome and Lee Yah used Absorb-Plus paper towels. Their graphs are shown here. Which paper towel can hold more water?

Student Guide - page 137

Homework

You will need a sheet of graph paper and a ruler to complete this homework.

1. Professor Peabody tested Whizzo brand paper towels. He noticed a very interesting pattern in his data. Then, his pet mouse, Milo, tracked ink across his data table. Look for a pattern in Professor Peabody's data.

N Number of Drops	A Area of Spot in sq cm
1	🐾🐾
2	🐾🐾
🐾🐾	8
8	16

A. Copy the data table on your paper and fill in the missing values.

B. Make a point graph of the data. Graph the number of drops on the horizontal axis and the area on the vertical axis. Use a ruler to fit a line to the points.

C. What would be the area of a spot made with no drops? Add this point to your graph.

2. A. Choose a point on the graph. Use it to write the ratio ($\frac{A}{N}$) of the area to the number of drops.

B. Using fractions, write two ratios equal to the ratio in Question 2A.

3. A. What area would 6 drops make on a Whizzo brand paper towel?

B. How many drops are needed to make a spot with an area of 28 sq cm? Show your work.

Student Guide - page 138

*Answers and/or discussion are included in the Lesson Guide.

Student Guide (pp. 137–138)

13. A. Using the sample graph in Figure 23, $\frac{14 \text{ sq cm}}{2 \text{ drops}}$. Answers will vary.*

B. Using the ratio in *Question 13A,* 84 sq cm.

C. Using the ratio in the answer to *Question 13A,* and a 28 cm by 23 cm piece of paper towel: 90–100 drops.*

14. Super Soak is more absorbent. It can hold the most water.*

Homework

1. A.

N Number of Drops	A Area of Spot in sq cm
1	2
2	4
4	8
8	16

B.

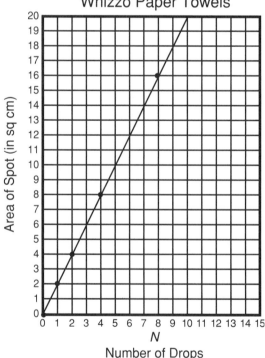

C. 0 sq cm

2. A. Answers will vary. $\frac{4 \text{ sq cm}}{2 \text{ drops}}$

B. Answers will vary. $\frac{16 \text{ sq cm}}{8 \text{ drops}}$, $\frac{20 \text{ sq cm}}{10 \text{ drops}}$

3. A. 12 sq cm

B. 14 drops

Discovery Assignment Book (p. 45)

Home Practice*

Part 4. Comparing Prices

1. Answers will vary. One possible ratio is $\frac{10¢}{2\ \text{pencils}}$.

2. Answers will vary. One possible ratio is $\frac{10¢}{1\ \text{pencil}}$.

3. Penny Pencils. One pencil costs 10¢ for Penny Pencils while 2 pencils cost 10¢ for Sharpy Pencils.

4. Penny Pencils

5. 20¢. Solution strategies will vary. Students might use the graph or use ratios:
$$\frac{10¢}{2\ \text{pencils}} = \frac{20¢}{4\ \text{pencils}}.$$

6. 6 pencils. Solution strategies will vary. Students might use the graph or use ratios.

7. 12 pencils. Solution strategies will vary. Students might use ratios. $\frac{30¢}{6\ \text{pencils}} = \frac{60¢}{12\ \text{pencils}}$.

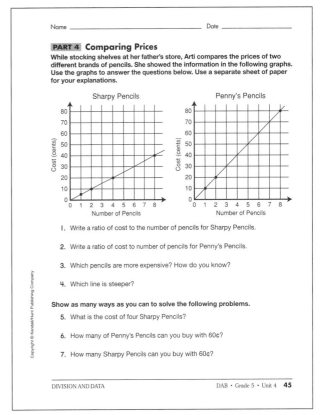

Name _____ Date _____

PART 4 Comparing Prices

While stocking shelves at her father's store, Arti compares the prices of two different brands of pencils. She showed the information in the following graphs. Use the graphs to answer the questions below. Use a separate sheet of paper for your explanations.

1. Write a ratio of cost to the number of pencils for Sharpy Pencils.

2. Write a ratio of cost to number of pencils for Penny's Pencils.

3. Which pencils are more expensive? How do you know?

4. Which line is steeper?

Show as many ways as you can to solve the following problems.

5. What is the cost of four Sharpy Pencils?

6. How many of Penny's Pencils can you buy with 60¢?

7. How many Sharpy Pencils can you buy with 60¢?

DIVISION AND DATA   DAB • Grade 5 • Unit 4   **45**

Discovery Assignment Book - page 45

---

*Answers for all the Home Practice in the *Discovery Assignment Book* are at the end of the unit.

Lesson 7

George Washington Carver: Man of Measure

Lesson Overview

Estimated Class Sessions

1

This story is based on actual historical events in the life of George Washington Carver. The story begins as George Washington Carver is visiting the World Columbian Exposition in Chicago in 1893. Carver is at the exposition because several of his paintings were selected to be displayed at the Iowa pavilion.

While at the exposition, Carver is torn between a love of painting and a deeply felt need to serve African Americans, his people. He spends much of his time studying the exhibits at the horticulture and agriculture buildings. These exhibits convince him of the power of scientific agriculture to improve the lives of poor southern farmers. They also help him choose a life devoted to the study of agriculture rather than the life of an artist. In a sense, this choice becomes one of the historical standards by which the life of George Washington Carver can be measured.

Carver is next seen about four years later as he struggles with one of the problems he must solve as Director of Agricultural Research at Tuskegee Institute. He doesn't have the necessary laboratory equipment to teach science and carry out research. Tuskegee Principal Booker T. Washington is unable to help Carver with the problem. Rather than give in to his frustration, Carver turns to his students for help. Together, they go to a local dump and gather containers and materials to use in setting up their science laboratory. While working with his students to prepare the materials they gathered, Carver discusses the ideas of variables, measuring, and standard units. Carver's students deepen their understandings of standard units and scientific measurement by making standard and other equipment used in scientific investigations.

Key Content

- Connecting mathematics and science to real-world events.
- Understanding the role of standard units in scientific measurement.

Key Vocabulary

- area
- graduated cylinder
- standard unit
- variable

Math Facts

Assign DPP item Z that reviews math facts using the order of operations.

Homework

Assign the *Variables* Activity Page.

Assessment

1. Have students draw up a plan for making a two-pan balance and use household items to build it.
2. Have students make their own standard masses.
3. Have students test the soil at school or home.

Curriculum Sequence

Before This Unit

Fundamental Variables

In kindergarten through fourth grade, students investigated these fundamental variables: length, area, mass, volume, and time in experiments and activities. In Unit 3 of fifth grade, students explored the relationship between distance (length) and time in the lab *Distance vs. Time.* In this unit, students explore area.

After This Unit

Fundamental Variables

In fifth grade, students explore the relationship between pairs of fundamental variables. For example, the ratio of distance (length) to time is defined as speed (Units 3 and 5), and the ratio of mass to volume is defined as density (Unit 13).

George Washington Carver

Another story about the life and work of George Washington Carver will appear in the Adventure Book *Peanut Soup* in Unit 12.

Materials List

Supplies and Copies

Student	Teacher
Supplies for Each Student	**Supplies**
Copies	**Copies/Transparencies**

All blackline masters including assessment, transparency, and DPP masters are also on the Teacher Resource CD.

Student Books

Variables (*Discovery Assignment Book* Page 67)
George Washington Carver: Man of Measure (*Adventure Book* Pages 21–34)

Daily Practice and Problems and Home Practice

DPP items Y–Z (*Unit Resource Guide* Pages 30–31)

Note: Classrooms whose pacing differs significantly from the suggested pacing of the units should use the Math Facts Calendar in Section 4 of the *Facts Resource Guide* to ensure students receive the complete math facts program.

Y. Bit: Medians and Means (URG p. 30)

In Language Arts, the students in Mr. Moreno's class are reading a novel together. Their homework each night is to continue reading the book. Every Monday each student reports the number of pages he or she read the week before. Jackie's data are shown below.

Day of the Week	Number of Pages
Monday	15
Tuesday	3
Wednesday	5
Thursday	7
Friday	20

1. What is the median number of pages Jackie read?
2. What is the mean number of pages Jackie read?
3. Which average would you use to represent the data? Why?

Z. Task: Order of Operations
(URG p. 31)

Solve each pair of problems and compare their answers.

A. $5 \times (7 - 2) =$

$5 \times 7 - 2 =$

B. $30 - 3 \times 7 =$

$(30 - 3) \times 7 =$

C. $18 \div 2 \times 3 =$

$18 \div (2 \times 3) =$

D. $(4 + 3) \times (8 + 2) =$

$4 + 3 \times 8 + 2 =$

"And Honorable Mention goes to Yucca and Cactus, painted by George Washington Carver!"

In 1893, at the World's Columbian Exposition in Chicago, a young artist named George Washington Carver watched in amazement and joy as his painting of a beautiful flowering cactus received an award. "Perhaps my dream of having a career as a painter will come true after all," he thought.

At that time, Carver was a college student, studying plants, at Iowa State University. However, many of his friends and teachers believed that he would eventually become a great artist. Carver himself had long felt that he had a special gift, but he knew that painting was only one of the many talents he possessed. Now he longed to feel certain about his life's work; he felt strongly that it was time for him to choose a path and follow it. But he was not so sure that painting was the path he was meant to follow.

Adventure Book - page 22

Page 22

- *What was the World Columbian Exposition and why is it important?*

The World Columbian Exposition was the 1893 World's Fair held in Chicago. The Columbian Exposition is of great historical significance because of the broad and powerful impact it exerted on a national and international scale. In many ways, the event represents a technological jump-start for the 20th century. Millions of people were exposed for the first time to scientific and technological advances like the electric light bulb.

"I could become a painter—but how much would that help my people?" Carver wondered. He was troubled by the problems faced by so many of his people, and his deepest wish was to be of service to them. Now, with all the wonders of agricultural science before him, he knew which career he should select. He could best serve his race by teaching them to farm. He would use the power of scientific agriculture to help his people—and all people.

Three years later in 1896, as a new teacher at Tuskegee Institute in Alabama, Carver was ready to explode with frustration. He wondered how he could possibly teach science without having a laboratory. He took his problem to the principal of the Institute, Booker T. Washington.

"Mr. Principal, this is impossible!" Carver exclaimed. "Even the school cook has better equipment than I do!"

Adventure Book - page 25

Page 25

- *What were the career paths that Carver wanted to pursue? How were they in conflict? On what principles or ideas did Carver base his decision to study agriculture?*

Carver was torn between painting and teaching agriculture. He based his decision to pursue a career in agriculture on his desire to be of service to African Americans.

Historical Note

Booker T. Washington wanted Carver to teach farmers how to increase their cotton production. Washington wanted the farmers to be able to make enough money to buy their own land and become self-sufficient. During the 19th and 20th centuries, cotton was both a profitable and high-risk commodity for farmers. When all went well, there was an enormous pay-off. But there were also many things, such as drought and boll weevils (a gray beetle that infests cotton plants), that can damage a field of cotton. Farmers who planted all their fields in cotton were taking a big gamble because if the cotton crop failed, they would have no money for essentials like food and housing.

Page 30

- *What are five variables Carver talks about in the story?*

Length, area, volume, mass, and time.

Students can use the *Variables* Activity Page in the *Discovery Assignment Book* to record and explore these variables. Encourage students to use examples from the story and from their experiences in laboratory investigations when filling in the table.

- *What are standard units of measure?*
- *Why do scientists need them?*

Standard units are specified quantities of a variable that are used in measuring that variable. Standard units are set and maintained on a national and international level. Standard units of measure are important to scientists because they need to communicate clearly what they measured and what they found. Without agreed-upon standards, this type of communication would be impossible.

George Washington Carver: Man of Measure

The next day in the classroom, with the pile of odd containers from the dump spread on a table, the students gathered around their teacher. Carver began, "Yesterday, Andrew asked why we need containers for measuring. Measuring variables is an important part of science. For instance, when scientists do experiments, they often need to measure variables such as length, area, volume, mass, and time."

"What do you mean by measuring a variable?" asked Herschel.

Carver thought for a moment and then replied, "Let's think about the five variables that I just named and how we measure them. We can start with time. What do we use to measure time, and what are its standard units?"

Herschel answered, "We measure time with a clock. Minutes are the units."

"Very good—but are there other standard units for time besides minutes?"

"Sure," answered Herschel. "There are seconds, hours, days, months . . ."

Carver noticed a hand waving in the back of the room. "Lydell, do you have a question?"

"Yes, sir. What's a standard unit, anyway?"

"Can anyone answer Lydell's question?"

30   AB • Grade 5 • Unit 4 • Lesson 7

Adventure Book - page 30

Name _____   Date _____

Variables

1. In *George Washington Carver: Man of Measure*, Professor Carver names five variables often used in math and science. Use these variables and Carver's discussion to fill in the table below.

Variable	Common Use (Example where the variable is used)	Standard Units	Equipment Needed for Measurement

2. Think of another variable that could be added to Professor Carver's list and add it to the data table.

George Washington Carver: Man of Measure   DAB • Grade 5 • Unit 4 • Lesson 7 **67**

Discovery Assignment Book - page 67 *(Answers on p. 143)*

"Great, James—we'll do that! You've got the right idea. We start with what we know—in this case, inches—and use them to make more yardsticks. Now let's think about measuring area. Can someone tell me exactly what area is?"

"Area is length times width," Herschel declared.

"Good try, Herschel, but length times width is actually a formula for measuring the area of a rectangle. Can someone explain the idea of area in words that aren't a formula?"

James raised his hand. "Isn't area the amount of surface it takes to cover something?"

"Excellent, James. Can you also tell me what are the standard units for measuring area?"

"That depends on what you're measuring," James replied. "We would use acres to measure a farm, but we would use other units to measure other things. For example, this table could be measured in square inches."

"And how would you measure the area of this table?" asked Carver.

"Like I said!" Herschel reminded the class. "It's the length in inches times the width in inches."

Carver laughed. "This time that's exactly right, Herschel. Now something else we need for the lab is a set of containers for measuring volume, which is the amount of space occupied by an object. Let's begin by making a container that will hold exactly 1 liter. How should we start?"

James answered in the way he thought his teacher would answer the question himself: "I think we should start with what we know."

"And what might that be?" asked Carver with a smile.

"Uh . . . I'm not sure," James admitted sheepishly.

Discussion Prompts

Page 32

- *Length times width is the formula for the area of a rectangle. How is the formula used in this story? Discuss the usefulness of the formula and its limitations. Discuss the difference between "area" and a formula for area.*

The formula is used to find the area of the lab table. **Area** can be defined as the amount of surface bound by a region or the amount of surface needed to cover something. Length × width is a formula for finding the area of a rectangle. The formula and area are distinct representations.

Carver pointed to the shelf behind him. "Why don't you look up here and see if you can find something that measures volume?"

"How about that skinny bottle with the lines on it?" asked James.

Carver took the graduated cylinder from the shelf. "Good—we can use this container for measuring volume. When we fill it up to the top line, it holds exactly 100 milliliters. So we call it a 100-milliliter graduated cylinder. Now can someone tell me how we can use this to make a 1-liter container?"

Herschel raised his hand. "Aren't there 1000 milliliters in one liter?"

Carver nodded. "That's right."

"So," Herschel said, "if we fill the graduated cylinder ten times and put all the water into one jar, we will have one liter, and then we can mark the level of 1 liter of water on the jar."

A few minutes later, Herschel proudly addressed his teacher. "We're finished, Professor Carver—here's our first 1-liter container!"

Page 33

- *Why did it take ten full graduated cylinders to make a 1-liter container?*

The graduated cylinder holds 100 ml when it is filled to the top line. Since 1 liter = 1000 ml, the graduated cylinder will need to be filled ten times to fill the larger container up to 1 liter.

Discussion Prompts

Page 34

- *Explain and elaborate on James's idea for making standard masses.*

James plans to use some tins he gathered that have lids to make standard masses. He plans to do this by filling the tins with the precise amount of sand needed to exactly balance them against the set of standard masses Carver brought from Iowa.

- *How did Professor Carver use the string he found at the dump?*

He used the string to make a balance from materials gathered at the dump.

Math Facts

DPP item Z uses the context of the order of operations to review math facts.

Homework and Practice

- Ask students to describe in words or pictures how each of the five variables discussed are measured in the story. Students can use the *Variables* Activity Page in the *Discovery Assignment Book* to organize their information. Descriptions should include all necessary equipment and the standard units used in the measurement.

- DPP Bit Y provides a quick review of medians and means.

Extension

- Draw up a plan for making a two-pan balance using common household items. Build it.

- Making the Standards: A Mass Measuring Activity

  Materials: A balance, a set of centimeter connecting cubes or standard masses, film canisters, or other similar closeable containers, sand, and masking tape.

  In this activity, students make 25-gram (or more) standard masses by filling film canisters with the amount of sand needed to balance them with 25 grams (or the desired amount). These home-made standard masses can be used in figuring the masses of heavier objects.

- Purchase inexpensive soil test kits and test soils around the school and at students' homes. How is the concept of volume used in these kits?

 George Washington Carver: Man of Measure

"Fine!" Carver answered. "We've gotten a good start on making standards for length, area, and volume. Now who has an idea about how to make standards to measure mass, which is the amount of matter in an object?"

James stood up. "I see something we could use to make a set of standard masses. Couldn't we use these little cans and fill them up with sand until they have the same mass as the standard ones?"

"That should work well," Carver said.

"But how can we know when they're the right mass?" Lydell asked.

"Look at what I've made, Lydell," directed Carver.

He reached into a cabinet and lifted out a balance made from pieces of wood, tin plates, and the untangled string. "With the materials we gathered from the dump and a clear understanding of how to measure mass, we can build enough balances for the whole class. We can use the balances to measure mass."

Through an understanding of science and measurement, Carver and his students were able to equip their first lab with the materials available to them. From this meager beginning, George Washington Carver went on to establish one of the most significant agricultural experimental stations of the twentieth century.

34   AB • Grade 5 • Unit 4 • Lesson 7

Adventure Book - page 34

 Historical Note

George Washington Carver was born in Diamond Grove, Missouri, around 1864. The date is not precisely known because Carver was born a slave. From this humble beginning, Carver went on to become a highly respected scientific thinker of the 20th century. After completing a master's degree in science at Iowa State in 1896, Carver moved to Alabama where he became Director of Agricultural Research at the Tuskegee Institute. He taught at Tuskegee and worked with poor Southern farmers until his death in 1943.

Literature Connections

- Adair, Gene. *George Washington Carver: Botanist.* Chelsea House Publishers, New York, 1989.

- Carter, Andy, and Carol Saller. *George Washington Carver.* Carolrhoda Books, Inc., Minneapolis, MN, 2001.

- Mitchel, Barbara. *A Pocketful of Goobers.* Carolrhoda Books, Inc., Minneapolis, MN, 1989.

- Moore, Eva. *The Story of George Washington Carver.* Scholastic, New York, 1995.

Resources

- Holt, Rackham. *George Washington Carver: An American Biography.* Doubleday, New York, 1961.

- Kremer, Gary R. *George Washington Carver: In His Own Words.* University of Missouri Press, Columbia, MO, 1987.

- McMurry, Linda L. *George Washington Carver: Scientist and Symbol.* Oxford University Press, New York, 1981.

Discovery Assignment Book (p. 67)

Variables

1.

Variable	Common Use (Example where the variable is used.)	Standard Units	Equipment Needed for Measurement
Length	pants size, waist and length	centimeters inches miles	ruler meterstick tape measure
Area	amount of carpet for floor	square in square cm	tiles ruler meterstick
Volume	measures for ingredients for cookies	cubic inches gallons liters	graduated cylinder cup liter
Mass	used to calculate the amount of fuel for the Space Shuttle	grams	balance
Time	used to measure the duration of an event	seconds minutes years	clock pendulum chronometer
Temperature Speed		degrees F or C length/time	

2. Two variables are listed in the data table as possible answers.

Name _____ Date _____

Variables

1. In *George Washington Carver: Man of Measure*, Professor Carver names five variables often used in math and science. Use these variables and Carver's discussion to fill in the table below.

Variable	Common Use (Example where the variable is used)	Standard Units	Equipment Needed for Measurement

2. Think of another variable that could be added to Professor Carver's list and add it to the data table.

George Washington Carver: Man of Measure   DAB • Grade 5 • Unit 4 • Lesson 7   **67**

Discovery Assignment Book - page 67

Review Problems

Lesson Overview

Estimated Class Sessions

1

Students complete a series of problems that review concepts in this and previous units. You can use these problems as a review for the midterm test.

Key Content

- Reviewing concepts and skills developed since the start of the year.
- Solving multistep word problems.
- Communicating solutions orally and in writing.
- Choosing appropriate methods and tools to calculate (calculator, pencil and paper, or mental math).
- Choosing to find an estimate or an exact answer.

Math Facts

Continue reviewing the multiplication and division facts for the square numbers.

Homework

1. Assign all or part of this lesson as homework.
2. Assign Part 5 of the Home Practice.

Materials List

Supplies and Copies

Student		Teacher	
Supplies for Each Student		**Supplies**	
• calculator • pattern blocks • ruler			
Copies		**Copies/Transparencies**	
• 2 copies of *Centimeter Graph Paper* per student (*Unit Resource Guide* Page 130)			

All blackline masters including assessment, transparency, and DPP masters are also on the Teacher Resource CD.

Student Books

Review Problems (*Student Guide* Pages 139–142)

Daily Practice and Problems and Home Practice

Home Practice Part 5 (*Discovery Assignment Book* Page 46)

Note: Classrooms whose pacing differs significantly from the suggested pacing of the units should use the Math Facts Calendar in Section 4 of the *Facts Resource Guide* to ensure students receive the complete math facts program.

Review Problems

Solve the following problems. Use tools that you feel are appropriate unless other directions are given. Record your solutions. Show any strategies that you used.

1. Lin traveled 7 miles during a hike. There are 5280 feet in 1 mile. How many feet did Lin travel?

2. John plays on a baseball team. He records the number of runs he scores each game. In the first five games of the season he scored 3, 0, 1, 1, and 5 runs.
   - **A.** Find the mean number of runs scored.
   - **B.** Find the median number of runs scored.
   - **C.** Which average, the median or the mean, better represents the number of runs John scored? Explain your choice.

3. One foot is equal to 12 inches.
   - **A.** Make a data table that compares feet to inches. Include at least 3 equal ratios.
   - **B.** Make a graph displaying your data. Put feet on the horizontal axis and inches on the vertical axis.

4. Use paper and pencil to solve these multiplication and division problems. Estimate to be sure your answers are reasonable.
   - **A.** $34 \times 56 =$
   - **B.** $1237 \times 9 =$
   - **C.** $567 \div 3 =$
   - **D.** $7954 \div 7 =$

5. Write the number 3×10^5 in standard form.

Student Guide - page 139 *(Answers on p. 149)*

Teaching the Activity

Use the problems in this review in class as part of a review session or assign them as homework to help students review concepts in previous units. The questions are structured to review the main concepts studied in Units 1–4. Evaluate students' work on each question to see if they need further practice or review before taking the *Midterm Test* in Lesson 9.

Students will need calculators, pattern blocks, rulers, *Centimeter Graph Paper,* and other tools to complete the questions. Remind students to follow the directions for each question. Some questions may ask for an estimate while others look for exact solutions. Also encourage students to select appropriately from the available tools. Remind students to give full explanations of their problem-solving strategies.

---

6. Jerome's mother is planning to re-tile the bathroom floor. The room measures 8 feet by 8 feet. She is planning to use square tiles that measure 6 inches by 6 inches.
   - **A.** What is the area of the bathroom floor?
   - **B.** How many tiles will she need? (*Hint:* Make a drawing.)

7. David plans to build a rectangular patio with 48 square tiles. Each tile has an area of 1 square foot. He does not want to cut the tiles, so the length and width of the patio must be whole numbers. What are all the possible measurements for the length and width of the patio?

8. Linda dumped out the change in her piggy bank. She arranged the change from her piggy bank into 9 piles of 83 coins each.
   - **A.** About how many coins does Linda have?
   - **B.** If all her coins were nickels, about how much money does she have?

Student Guide - page 140 *(Answers on p. 149)*

---

9. What is the value of the 5 in 345,687?

10. Use this pattern block to answer the following questions.
    - **A.** Draw one whole.
    - **B.** Draw one-half.
    - **C.** Draw two-thirds.
    - **D.** Draw five-sixths.

11. Jessie has a bag of tiles. She pulls a sample of tiles from her bag. Her data are shown below. Draw a graph to display her data.

C Color	N Number of Tiles Pulled
Red	6
Blue	6
Green	5
Yellow	3

   - **A.** What is the most common color(s) in Jessie's sample?
   - **B.** What is the least common color(s) in Jessie's sample?
   - **C.** How many tiles are in Jessie's sample?
   - **D.** What fraction of the tiles Jessie pulled are blue?
   - **E.** Jessie took her sample from a bag of 200 tiles. Use her sample to predict the total number of tiles of each color. Explain your reasoning.

Student Guide - page 141 *(Answers on p. 150)*

- Assign all or part of the questions for homework.
- Assign Part 5 of the Home Practice that includes more practice problems.

Answers for Part 5 of the Home Practice are in the Answer Key at the end of this lesson and the end of this unit.

---

12. Compare the following fractions. Tell which is greater. Write a number sentence to show your answer. Use the symbols < and > in your answer.
    A. $\frac{3}{4}$ or $\frac{6}{5}$
    B. $\frac{4}{9}$ or $\frac{5}{9}$
    C. $\frac{3}{6}$ or $\frac{3}{7}$

13. Estimate the answers to the following problems.
    A. $346,000 \times 5$
    B. $251,000 \times 7$
    C. $51,000 \times 5$

Solve the following problems.

14. A. $81 \div 9 =$
    B. $810 \div 9 =$
    C. $810 \div 90 =$
    D. $8100 \div 9 =$
    E. $8100 \div 90 =$
    F. $8100 \div 900 =$

15. Use paper and pencil to divide. Estimate to check if your answer is reasonable.
    A. $5\overline{)756}$ B. $4\overline{)1596}$ C. $8\overline{)6407}$

16. A. $36 \div (3 \times 3) =$ B. $36 \div 3 \times 3 =$
    C. $36 \div (4 + 2) =$ D. $36 \div 4 + 2 =$

Student Guide - page 142 *(Answers on p. 151)*

Name _____ Date _____

PART 5 Word Problems

Solve the following problems. Choose an appropriate method for each: mental math, paper and pencil, or a calculator. Explain your solutions. Use a separate sheet of paper to show your work.

1. Mighty Tree Tree Farm is having a sale. Seedlings (very young trees) are grouped in bunches of 15 for $25.00, tax included. Coleman School decided to buy 6 bunches to plant on the school grounds.
   A. How many seedlings did Coleman School buy?

   B. How much money did Coleman School spend?

2. Mr. Moreno's class volunteered to plant the seedlings on the school grounds. There are 22 students present in Mr. Moreno's class on planting day. If each student plants about the same number of seedlings, how many seedlings will each student plant?

3. Mighty Tree Tree Farm also sells older trees. They charge $8.00 per foot in height for older trees, tax included. Jacob's family chooses to buy two trees that are the same height. The total cost is $128. How tall are the two trees?

4. Once a year, Mighty Tree Tree Farm has a Truckload Bargain Day. On this day, customers pay $250 and get a truckload of trees. One truckload has 9 trees. Estimate the cost of one tree in this truckload.

5. This year, Mighty Tree Tree Farm sold 32 truckloads at $250 each. How much money did Mighty Tree Tree Farm take in on this day?

6. Last year, Mighty Tree Tree Farm sold 450 trees on Truckload Bargain Day. If each truckload contained 9 trees, how many truckloads did they sell?

7. Alexis is at the tree farm with her sister and her father. They wish to purchase a tree to plant in their backyard. They like five different kinds of trees. The heights of the trees they like are: 3 feet, 4 feet, 5 feet, 2 feet, and 6 feet.
   A. If they choose the tree with the median height, which tree would they choose?

   B. What is the mean height of the five trees they like?

Discovery Assignment Book - page 46 *(Answers on p. 151)*

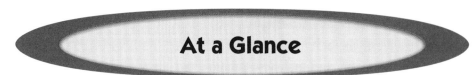

At a Glance

Math Facts and Daily Practice and Problems

Continue reviewing the multiplication and division facts for the square numbers.

Teaching the Activity

Students complete a variety of problems that review concepts learned in this and previous units as homework or a class review. Have available calculators, pattern blocks, rulers, *Centimeter Graph Paper,* and other tools.

Homework

1. Assign all or part of this lesson as homework.
2. Assign Part 5 of the Home Practice.

Answer Key is on pages 149–151.

Notes:

Student Guide (pp. 139–140)

Review Problems

1. 36,960 feet

2. **A.** 2 runs

   B. 1 run

   C. Answers will vary. The mean may represent the data better. Using the median, the 5 runs are not considered. This question illustrates that averages are subject to interpretation.

3. **A.**

Feet and Inches

Feet	Inches
1	12
2	24
3	36

   B.

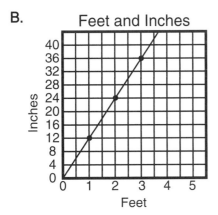

4. **A.** 1904

   B. 11,133

   C. 189

   D. 1136 R2

5. 300,000

6. **A.** 64 square feet

   B. 256 tiles

7. Possible measurements: 1 foot by 48 feet, 2 feet by 24 feet, 3 feet by 16 feet, 4 feet by 12 feet, and 6 feet by 8 feet. Some students might say that 1 foot by 48 feet is not reasonable since the patio would be very narrow.

8. **A.** Estimates will vary; $9 \times 80 = 720$ coins.

   B. About $36

Review Problems

Solve the following problems. Use tools that you feel are appropriate unless other directions are given. Record your solutions. Show any strategies that you used.

1. Lin traveled 7 miles during a hike. There are 5280 feet in 1 mile. How many feet did Lin travel?

2. John plays on a baseball team. He records the number of runs he scores each game. In the first five games of the season he scored 3, 0, 1, 1, and 5 runs.
   A. Find the mean number of runs scored.
   B. Find the median number of runs scored.
   C. Which average, the median or the mean, better represents the number of runs John scored? Explain your choice.

3. One foot is equal to 12 inches.
   A. Make a data table that compares feet to inches. Include at least 3 equal ratios.
   B. Make a graph displaying your data. Put feet on the horizontal axis and inches on the vertical axis.

4. Use paper and pencil to solve these multiplication and division problems. Estimate to be sure your answers are reasonable.
   A. $34 \times 56 =$ **B.** $1237 \times 9 =$
   C. $567 \div 3 =$ **D.** $7954 \div 7 =$

5. Write the number 3×10^5 in standard form.

Review Problems   SG • Grade 5 • Unit 4 • Lesson 8   **139**

Student Guide - page 139

6. Jerome's mother is planning to re-tile the bathroom floor. The room measures 8 feet by 8 feet. She is planning to use square tiles that measure 6 inches by 6 inches.
   A. What is the area of the bathroom floor?
   B. How many tiles will she need? (Hint: Make a drawing.)

7. David plans to build a rectangular patio with 48 square tiles. Each tile has an area of 1 square foot. He does not want to cut the tiles, so the length and width of the patio must be whole numbers. What are all the possible measurements for the length and width of the patio?

8. Linda dumped out the change in her piggy bank. She arranged the change from her piggy bank into 9 piles of 83 coins each.
   A. About how many coins does Linda have?
   B. If all her coins were nickels, about how much money does she have?

140 SG • Grade 5 • Unit 4 • Lesson 8   Review Problems

Student Guide - page 140

9. What is the value of the 5 in 345,687?

10. Use this pattern block to answer the following questions.
    A. Draw one whole.
    B. Draw one-half.
    C. Draw two-thirds.
    D. Draw five-sixths.

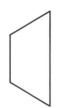

11. Jessie has a bag of tiles. She pulls a sample of tiles from her bag. Her data are shown below. Draw a graph to display her data.

C Color	N Number of Tiles Pulled
Red	6
Blue	6
Green	5
Yellow	3

A. What is the most common color(s) in Jessie's sample?
B. What is the least common color(s) in Jessie's sample?
C. How many tiles are in Jessie's sample?
D. What fraction of the tiles Jessie pulled are blue?
E. Jessie took her sample from a bag of 200 tiles. Use her sample to predict the total number of tiles of each color. Explain your reasoning.

Student Guide - page 141

Student Guide (p. 141)

9. 5000

10. **A.** One solution is:

B.

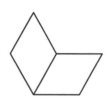

C.

D.

11. An appropriate graph is a bar graph as shown.

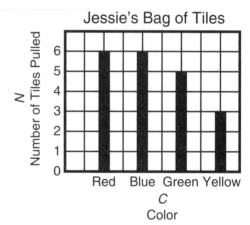

A. red and blue   **B.** yellow
C. 20 tiles   **D.** $\frac{6}{20}$ or $\frac{3}{10}$

E. 60 red, 60 blue, 50 green, 30 yellow

Possible explanation: There are 20 tiles in the sample and 200 tiles in the bag. So there are $200 \div 20$, or 10 times as many tiles in the bag as the sample. So I multiplied the number of tiles of each color in the sample by 10.

Student Guide (p. 142)

12. A. $\frac{6}{5}; \frac{6}{5} > \frac{3}{4}$

   B. $\frac{5}{9}; \frac{5}{9} > \frac{4}{9}$

   C. $\frac{3}{6}; \frac{3}{6} > \frac{3}{7}$

13. A. $350,000 \times 5 = 1,750,000$

   B. $250,000 \times 7 = 1,750,000$

   C. $50,000 \times 5 = 250,000$

14. A. 9   **B.** 90

   C. 9   **D.** 900

   E. 90   **F.** 9

15. A. 151 R1

   B. 399

   C. 800 R7

16. A. 4   **B.** 36

   C. 6   **D.** 11

---

12. Compare the following fractions. Tell which is greater. Write a number sentence to show your answer. Use the symbols < and > in your answer.

   A. $\frac{3}{4}$ or $\frac{6}{5}$

   B. $\frac{4}{9}$ or $\frac{5}{9}$

   C. $\frac{3}{6}$ or $\frac{3}{7}$

13. Estimate the answers to the following problems.

   A. $346,000 \times 5$

   B. $251,000 \times 7$

   C. $51,000 \times 5$

Solve the following problems.

14. A. $81 \div 9 =$

   B. $810 \div 9 =$

   C. $810 \div 90 =$

   D. $8100 \div 9 =$

   E. $8100 \div 90 =$

   F. $8100 \div 900 =$

15. Use paper and pencil to divide. Estimate to check if your answer is reasonable.

   A. $5\overline{)756}$ **B.** $4\overline{)1596}$ **C.** $8\overline{)6407}$

16. A. $36 \div (3 \times 3) =$ **B.** $36 \div 3 \times 3 =$

   C. $36 \div (4 + 2) =$ **D.** $36 \div 4 + 2 =$

Student Guide - page 142

Discovery Assignment Book (p. 46)

Home Practice*

Part 5. Word Problems

1. A. 90 seedlings

   B. $150.00

2. 4 seedlings each with 2 left over

3. 8 feet each

4. About $25; $250 \div 10 = 25

5. $8000

6. 50 truckloads

7. A. 4 feet

   B. 4 feet

Name _____ Date _____

PART 5 Word Problems

Solve the following problems. Choose an appropriate method for each: mental math, paper and pencil, or a calculator. Explain your solutions. Use a separate sheet of paper to show your work.

1. Mighty Tree Tree Farm is having a sale. Seedlings (very young trees) are grouped in bunches of 15 for $25.00, tax included. Coleman School decided to buy 6 bunches to plant on the school grounds.
   A. How many seedlings did Coleman School buy?

   B. How much money did Coleman School spend?

2. Mr. Moreno's class volunteered to plant the seedlings on the school grounds. There are 22 students present in Mr. Moreno's class on planting day. If each student plants about the same number of seedlings, how many seedlings will each student plant?

3. Mighty Tree Tree Farm also sells older trees. They charge $8.00 per foot in height for older trees, tax included. Jacob's family chooses to buy two trees that are the same height. The total cost is $128. How tall are the two trees?

4. Once a year, Mighty Tree Tree Farm has a Truckload Bargain Day. On this day, customers pay $250 and get a truckload of trees. One truckload has 9 trees. Estimate the cost of one tree in this truckload.

5. This year, Mighty Tree Tree Farm sold 32 truckloads at $250 each. How much money did Mighty Tree Tree Farm take in on this day?

6. Last year, Mighty Tree Tree Farm sold 450 trees on Truckload Bargain Day. If each truckload contained 9 trees, how many truckloads did they sell?

7. Alexis is at the tree farm with her sister and her father. They wish to purchase a tree to plant in their backyard. They like five different kinds of trees. The heights of the trees they like are: 3 feet, 4 feet, 5 feet, 2 feet, and 6 feet.
   A. If they choose the tree with the median height, which tree would they choose?

   B. What is the mean height of the five trees they like?

Discovery Assignment Book - page 46

*Answers for all the Home Practice in the *Discovery Assignment Book* are at the end of the unit.

Lesson 9

Midterm Test

Lesson Overview

Students take a paper-and-pencil test consisting of items that test skills and concepts studied in the first four units.

Key Content

- Assessing concepts and skills developed since the start of the year.

Math Facts

Assign DPP item AA.

Materials List

Supplies and Copies

Student	Teacher
Supplies for Each Student • calculator • pattern blocks • ruler	**Supplies**
Copies • 2 copies of *Centimeter Graph Paper* per student (*Unit Resource Guide* Page 130) • 1 copy of *Midterm Test* per student (*Unit Resource Guide* Pages 156–161)	**Copies/Transparencies**

All blackline masters including assessment, transparency, and DPP masters are also on the Teacher Resource CD.

Daily Practice and Problems and Home Practice

DPP items AA–BB (*Unit Resource Guide* Page 31)

Note: Classrooms whose pacing differs significantly from the suggested pacing of the units should use the Math Facts Calendar in Section 4 of the *Facts Resource Guide* to ensure students receive the complete math facts program.

Daily Practice and Problems

Suggestions for using the DPPs are below.

AA. Bit: Quiz: Square Numbers
(URG p. 31)

A. $5 \times 5 =$

B. $4 \div 2 =$

C. $81 \div 9 =$

D. $10 \times 10 =$

E. $8 \times 8 =$

F. $16 \div 4 =$

G. $9 \div 3 =$

H. $6 \times 6 =$

I. $49 \div 7 =$

BB. Challenge: Collecting Data
(URG p. 31)

How many sit-ups can you do in one minute? Collect data from your classmates. One student in each pair can take turns being the timekeeper. Once you collect the data, find the median and mean number of sit-ups the students in your sample can do.

Teaching the Assessment

Students take this test individually. It was designed to be completed in 1–2 class sessions. Part 1 consists of *Questions 1–6,* which assess students' estimation skills and fluency with multidigit multiplication and division. Students should complete this part of the test without a calculator. Students need a ruler, a calculator, and pattern blocks to complete Part 2 of the test. They need graph paper to complete *Questions 7–8.*

Students should follow the directions given for each question. Remind students to give full explanations of their problem-solving strategies when asked.

Math Facts

DPP item AA is a quiz on the multiplication and division facts for the square numbers.

Extension

Assign DPP Challenge BB, which reviews averages.

Estimated Class Sessions **1-2**

Math Facts and Daily Practice and Problems

Assign items AA–BB.

Teaching the Assessment

1. Students complete Part 1 of the test *(Questions 1–6)* without using a calculator.
2. Students complete Part 2 of the test using calculators, rulers, graph paper, and pattern blocks.

Extension

Assign DPP Challenge BB.

Answer Key is on pages 162–164.

Notes:

Midterm Test

Part 1

Solve the following problems without using a calculator. Remember to check if your answers are reasonable.

1. $\begin{array}{r} 87 \\ \times 63 \\ \hline \end{array}$

2. $\begin{array}{r} 4169 \\ \times 7 \\ \hline \end{array}$

3. $9\overline{)3717}$

4. $3\overline{)2567}$

5. **Estimate** the answers to the following problems.

   A. $526{,}000 \times 40$

   B. 8350×20

6. Tell the value of the 4 in each of the following numbers.

   A. 4329

   B. 262,578,413

   C. 4,009,002

   D. 42,613

Assessment Blackline Master

Part 2

To answer Questions 7–14, you will need two sheets of graph paper. You may use any tools that you used in class. For example, you may use a ruler, pattern blocks, or a calculator.

7. The students in Mrs. Wells's classroom collected data on the number of buttons on their clothing. Here are the data they collected:

B Buttons	N Number of Students	
	Tallies	Total
0	~~||||~~ ||||	9
1	~~||||~~	5
2					3
3					3
4			1
5				2
6		0
7			1
8		0
9		0
10					3

A. Make a graph of the data.

B. How many students were in Mrs. Wells's room when the data were gathered? _____

C. What was the most common number (mode) of buttons on this day?

_____

D. What was the median number of buttons on this day? Show your thinking.

8. Edward and Nicholas went to the snack stand at the park. They saw that they could purchase 2 Ice Pops for 30¢.

    A. Use this information to complete the following table.

Number of Ice Pops	Cost
1	
2	30¢
3	
4	
5	

    B. Make a graph that compares the cost of Ice Pops to the number of Ice Pops. Plot the number of Ice Pops on the horizontal axis and the cost on the vertical axis.

    C. Use fractions to write three ratios equal to $\frac{30¢}{2 \text{ Ice Pops}}$.

Assessment Blackline Master

9. Estimate the area of the following shapes. Explain your strategy for each one.

A.

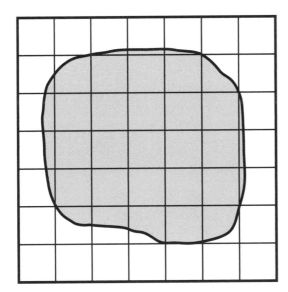

B.

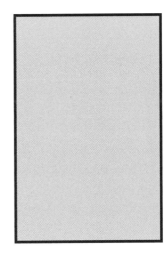

A. Area = _____

Strategy:

B. Area = _____

Strategy:

10. Rewrite this number in standard notation: 5.68×10^6.

_____

11. Use this pattern block to answer the following questions. Show your work. Be sure to label your work clearly.

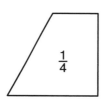

    A. Draw one whole.

    B. Draw three-fourths.

    C. Draw five-sixths.

    D. Draw six-fourths.

Assessment Blackline Master

12. Write two number sentences for the pattern blocks shown below. The yellow hexagon is one whole.

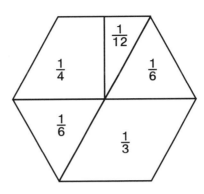

13. Complete the number sentences:

A. $\frac{15}{20} = \frac{?}{4}$ **B.** $\frac{7}{8} = \frac{?}{24}$

14. Write a number sentence to show which fraction is larger. Explain the strategies you used. Use the symbols $<$ and $>$ in your answer.

A. $\frac{2}{10}$ or $\frac{3}{4}$

B. $\frac{3}{7}$ or $\frac{4}{7}$

C. $\frac{5}{8}$ or $\frac{5}{9}$

Name _____ Date _____

Midterm Test

Part 1

Solve the following problems without using a calculator. Remember to check if your answers are reasonable.

1. $\begin{array}{r} 87 \\ \times 63 \\ \hline \end{array}$　　　　2. $\begin{array}{r} 4169 \\ \times 7 \\ \hline \end{array}$

3. $9\overline{)3717}$　　　　4. $3\overline{)2567}$

5. **Estimate** the answers to the following problems.
   A. $526{,}000 \times 40$

   B. 8350×20

6. Tell the value of the 4 in each of the following numbers.
   A. 4329　　　　B. 262,578,413

   C. 4,009,002　　　　D. 42,613

Unit Resource Guide - page 156

Unit Resource Guide (p. 156)

Midterm Test

1. 5481

2. 29,183

3. 413

4. 855 R2

5. A. Estimates will vary. One possible estimate is $500{,}000 \times 40 = 20{,}000{,}000$.

   B. Estimates will vary. One possible estimate is $8000 \times 20 = 160{,}000$.

6. A. 4000

   B. 400

   C. 4,000,000

   D. 40,000

Name _____ Date _____

Part 2

To answer Questions 7–14, you will need two sheets of graph paper. You may use any tools that you used in class. For example, you may use a ruler, pattern blocks, or a calculator.

7. The students in Mrs. Wells's classroom collected data on the number of buttons on their clothing. Here are the data they collected:

B Buttons	N Number of Students	
	Tallies	Total
0	卌 IIII	9
1	卌	5
2	III	3
3	III	3
4	I	1
5	II	2
6		0
7	I	1
8		0
9		0
10	III	3

A. Make a graph of the data.
B. How many students were in Mrs. Wells's room when the data were gathered? _____
C. What was the most common number (mode) of buttons on this day?
_____

Unit Resource Guide - page 157

Unit Resource Guide (p. 157)

7. A. An appropriate graph is a bar graph as shown.

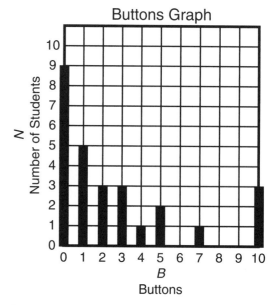

Buttons Graph

B. 27 students　　　C. 0 buttons

D. 1 button. Since there are 27 students, the median is between the 13th and 14th value which is 1.

Unit Resource Guide (p. 158)

8. A.

Number of Ice Pops	Cost
1	15¢
2	30¢
3	45¢
4	60¢
5	75¢

B.

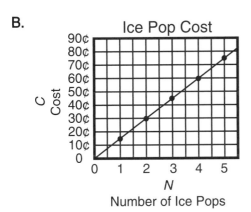

C. Ratios will vary. Three possible ratios are:

$$\frac{15¢}{1 \text{ Ice pop}}, \frac{45¢}{3 \text{ Ice Pops}}, \frac{60¢}{4 \text{ Ice Pops}}.$$

Unit Resource Guide (p. 159)

9. A. 24–25 sq cm. Strategies will vary. One possible strategy is to count and piece together square centimeters.

   B. 24 sq cm. Strategies will vary. One possible strategy is to measure the lengths of the sides and multiply: 6 cm × 4 cm = 24 sq cm.

10. 5,680,000

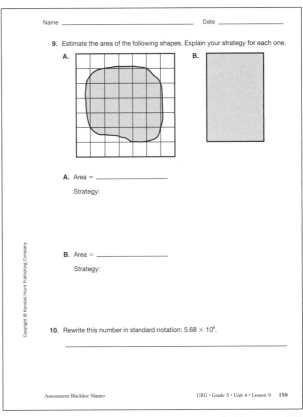

Name _____ Date _____

D. What was the median number of buttons on this day? Show your thinking.

8. Edward and Nicholas went to the snack stand at the park. They saw that they could purchase 2 Ice Pops for 30¢.

   A. Use this information to complete the following table.

Number of Ice Pops	Cost
1	
2	30¢
3	
4	
5	

   B. Make a graph that compares the cost of Ice Pops to the number of Ice Pops. Plot the number of Ice Pops on the horizontal axis and the cost on the vertical axis.

   C. Use fractions to write three ratios equal to $\frac{30¢}{2 \text{ Ice Pops}}$.

158   URG • Grade 5 • Unit 4 • Lesson 9   Assessment Blackline Master

Unit Resource Guide - page 158

Name _____ Date _____

9. Estimate the area of the following shapes. Explain your strategy for each one.

   A.   B.

   A. Area = _____
   Strategy:

   B. Area = _____
   Strategy:

   10. Rewrite this number in standard notation: 5.68×10^6.

   _____

Assessment Blackline Master   URG • Grade 5 • Unit 4 • Lesson 9   159

Unit Resource Guide - page 159

Name _____ Date _____

11. Use this pattern block to answer the following questions. Show your work. Be sure to label your work clearly.

A. Draw one whole.

B. Draw three-fourths.

C. Draw five-sixths.

D. Draw six-fourths.

Assessment Blackline Master

Copyright © Kendall/Hunt Publishing Company

Unit Resource Guide - page 160

Name _____ Date _____

12. Write two number sentences for the pattern blocks shown below. The yellow hexagon is one whole.

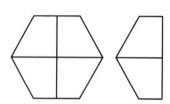

13. Complete the number sentences:

A. $\frac{15}{20} = \frac{?}{4}$ B. $\frac{7}{8} = \frac{?}{24}$

14. Write a number sentence to show which fraction is larger. Explain the strategies you used. Use the symbols < and > in your answer.

A. $\frac{2}{10}$ or $\frac{3}{4}$

B. $\frac{3}{7}$ or $\frac{4}{7}$

C. $\frac{5}{8}$ or $\frac{5}{9}$

Copyright © Kendall/Hunt Publishing Company

Assessment Blackline Master   URG • Grade 5 • Unit 4 • Lesson 9   **161**

Unit Resource Guide - page 161

Unit Resource Guide (p. 160)

11. A.

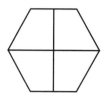

B.

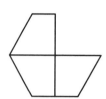

C.

D.

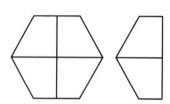

Unit Resource Guide (p. 161)

12. Number sentences will vary. Two possible number sentences include:

$\frac{1}{4} + \frac{1}{12} + \frac{1}{6} + \frac{1}{3} + \frac{1}{6} = 1$ and $\frac{1}{4} + \frac{1}{12} + \frac{2}{6} + \frac{1}{3} = 1$.

13. A. $\frac{15}{20} = \frac{3}{4}$

B. $\frac{7}{8} = \frac{21}{24}$

14. Strategies will vary.

A. $\frac{3}{4} > \frac{2}{10}$

B. $\frac{4}{7} > \frac{3}{7}$

C. $\frac{5}{8} > \frac{5}{9}$

Discovery Assignment Book (p. 43)

Part 2. Area

1. 100 square feet

2. 1440 square centimeters

3. About 5 times greater

4. **A.** 96 square feet

   B. Yes, if the backyard is 8 feet by 12.5 feet or $8\frac{1}{3}$ feet by 12 feet.

Name _____ Date _____

Unit 4 Home Practice

PART 1 *Triangle Flash Cards: Square Numbers*
Study for the quiz on the multiplication and division facts for the square numbers. Take home your *Triangle Flash Cards: Square Numbers* and your list of facts you need to study.

To quiz a multiplication fact, cover the corner containing the highest number. Multiply the two uncovered numbers.

To quiz a division fact, cover one of the smaller numbers. Use the two uncovered numbers to solve a division fact.

Mix up the multiplication and division facts. Sometimes cover the highest number and sometimes cover a smaller number.

Your teacher will tell you when the quiz on the square numbers will be given.

PART 2 Area
Solve the following problems. Choose an appropriate method for each: mental math, paper and pencil, or a calculator. Explain your solutions. Use a separate sheet of paper to show your work.

1. Jessie's parents are buying a rug for Jessie's bedroom. Jessie measured the length and width of her bedroom floor. It is 10 feet by 10 feet. What is the area of her bedroom floor?

2. Arti is putting together a jigsaw puzzle. The finished puzzle is 36 cm by 40 cm. What is the area of the puzzle?

3. Jerome's grandmother has an 8-inch by 10-inch wedding picture of herself and Jerome's grandfather. Her wedding picture sits next to Jerome's 3-inch by 5-inch school picture. About how many times greater in area is the wedding picture than the school picture?

4. **A.** Nila's older sister has a dog run for her dog in the backyard. The run is 12 feet by 8 feet. What is the area of the dog run?

   B. Nila wants to put the same size dog run in her backyard. If her backyard is 100 square feet, will an 8 feet by 12 feet dog run fit?

DIVISION AND DATA   DAB • Grade 5 • Unit 4   **43**

Discovery Assignment Book - page 43

Discovery Assignment Book (p. 44)

Part 3. Multiplication and Division Practice

A. 441

B. 22 R3

C. 810

D. 266

E. 1672

F. 944 R2

G. 1215

H. 3189

I. 7576

J. 965

K. 14,760

L. 1614

Name _____ Date _____

PART 3 Multiplication and Division Practice
Solve the following problems using a paper-and-pencil method. Estimate to be sure your answers are reasonable.

A. $49 \times 9 =$ B. $135 \div 6 =$ C. $18 \times 45 =$ D. $1064 \div 4 =$

E. $22 \times 76 =$ F. $2834 \div 3 =$ G. $8505 \div 7 =$ H. $1063 \times 3 =$

I. $1894 \times 4 =$ J. $7720 \div 8 =$ K. $2460 \times 6 =$ L. $8070 \div 5 =$

44 DAB • Grade 5 • Unit 4   DIVISION AND DATA

Discovery Assignment Book - page 44

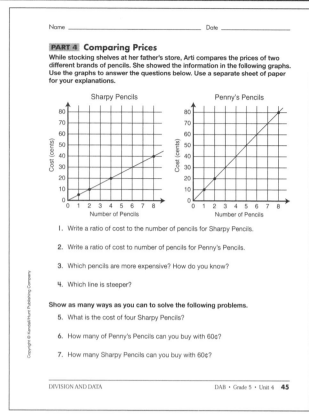

Name _____ Date _____

PART 4 Comparing Prices

While stocking shelves at her father's store, Arti compares the prices of two different brands of pencils. She showed the information in the following graphs. Use the graphs to answer the questions below. Use a separate sheet of paper for your explanations.

Sharpy Pencils

Penny's Pencils

1. Write a ratio of cost to the number of pencils for Sharpy Pencils.

2. Write a ratio of cost to number of pencils for Penny's Pencils.

3. Which pencils are more expensive? How do you know?

4. Which line is steeper?

Show as many ways as you can to solve the following problems.

5. What is the cost of four Sharpy Pencils?

6. How many of Penny's Pencils can you buy with 60¢?

7. How many Sharpy Pencils can you buy with 60¢?

DIVISION AND DATA   DAB • Grade 5 • Unit 4   **45**

Discovery Assignment Book - page 45

Discovery Assignment Book (p. 45)

Part 4. Comparing Prices

1. Answers will vary. One possible ratio is $\frac{10¢}{2 \text{ pencils}}$.

2. Answers will vary. One possible ratio is $\frac{10¢}{1 \text{ pencil}}$.

3. Penny Pencils. One pencil costs 10¢ for Penny Pencils while 2 pencils cost 10¢ for Sharpy Pencils.

4. Penny Pencils

5. 20¢. Solution strategies will vary. Students might use the graph or use ratios: $\frac{10¢}{2 \text{ pencils}} = \frac{20¢}{4 \text{ pencils}}$.

6. 6 pencils. Solution strategies will vary. Students might use the graph or use ratios.

7. 12 pencils. Solution strategies will vary. Students might use ratios. $\frac{30¢}{6 \text{ pencils}} = \frac{60¢}{12 \text{ pencils}}$.

Name _____ Date _____

PART 5 Word Problems

Solve the following problems. Choose an appropriate method for each: mental math, paper and pencil, or a calculator. Explain your solutions. Use a separate sheet of paper to show your work.

1. Mighty Tree Tree Farm is having a sale. Seedlings (very young trees) are grouped in bunches of 15 for $25.00, tax included. Coleman School decided to buy 6 bunches to plant on the school grounds.
   A. How many seedlings did Coleman School buy?

   B. How much money did Coleman School spend?

2. Mr. Moreno's class volunteered to plant the seedlings on the school grounds. There are 22 students present in Mr. Moreno's class on planting day. If each student plants about the same number of seedlings, how many seedlings will each student plant?

3. Mighty Tree Tree Farm also sells older trees. They charge $8.00 per foot in height for older trees, tax included. Jacob's family chooses to buy two trees that are the same height. The total cost is $128. How tall are the two trees?

4. Once a year, Mighty Tree Tree Farm has a Truckload Bargain Day. On this day, customers pay $250 and get a truckload of trees. One truckload has 9 trees. Estimate the cost of one tree in this truckload.

5. This year, Mighty Tree Tree Farm sold 32 truckloads at $250 each. How much money did Mighty Tree Tree Farm take in on this day?

6. Last year, Mighty Tree Tree Farm sold 450 trees on Truckload Bargain Day. If each truckload contained 9 trees, how many truckloads did they sell?

7. Alexis is at the tree farm with her sister and her father. They wish to purchase a tree to plant in their backyard. They like five different kinds of trees. The heights of the trees they like are: 3 feet, 4 feet, 5 feet, 2 feet, and 6 feet.
   A. If they choose the tree with the median height, which tree would they choose?

   B. What is the mean height of the five trees they like?

46 DAB • Grade 5 • Unit 4   DIVISION AND DATA

Discovery Assignment Book - page 46

Discovery Assignment Book (p. 46)

Part 5. Word Problems

1. A. 90 seedlings
   B. $150.00

2. 4 seedlings each with 2 left over

3. 8 feet each

4. About $25; $250 ÷ 10 = $25

5. $8000

6. 50 truckloads

7. A. 4 feet
   B. 4 feet

Glossary

This glossary provides definitions of key vocabulary terms in the Grade 5 lessons. Locations of key vocabulary terms in the curriculum are included with each definition. Components Key: URG = *Unit Resource Guide* and SG = *Student Guide.*

A

Acute Angle (URG Unit 6; SG Unit 6)
An angle that measures less than 90º.

Acute Triangle (URG Unit 6 & Unit 15; SG Unit 6 & Unit 15)
A triangle that has only acute angles.

All-Partials Multiplication Method (URG Unit 2)
A paper-and-pencil method for solving multiplication problems. Each partial product is recorded on a separate line. (*See also* partial product.)

$$
\begin{array}{r}
186 \\
\times\ 3 \\
\hline
18 \\
240 \\
300 \\
\hline
558
\end{array}
$$

Altitude of a Triangle (URG Unit 15; SG Unit 15)
A line segment from a vertex of a triangle perpendicular to the opposite side or to the line extending the opposite side; also, the length of this line. The altitude is also called the height of the triangle.

Angle (URG Unit 6; SG Unit 6)
The amount of turning or the amount of opening between two rays that have the same endpoint.

Arc (URG Unit 14; SG Unit 14)
Part of a circle between two points. (*See also* circle.)

Area (URG Unit 4 & Unit 15; SG Unit 4 & Unit 15)
A measurement of size. The area of a shape is the amount of space it covers, measured in square units.

Average (URG Unit 1 & Unit 4; SG Unit 1 & Unit 4)
A number that can be used to represent a typical value in a set of data. (*See also* mean, median, and mode.)

Axes (URG Unit 10; SG Unit 10)
Reference lines on a graph. In the Cartesian coordinate system, the axes are two perpendicular lines that meet at the origin. The singular of axes is axis.

B

Base of a Triangle (URG Unit 15; SG Unit 15)
One of the sides of a triangle; also, the length of the side. A perpendicular line drawn from the vertex opposite the base is called the height or altitude of the triangle.

Base of an Exponent (URG Unit 2; SG Unit 2)
When exponents are used, the number being multiplied. In $3^4 = 3 \times 3 \times 3 \times 3 = 81$, the 3 is the base and the 4 is the exponent. The 3 is multiplied by itself 4 times.

Base-Ten Pieces (URG Unit 2; SG Unit 2)
A set of manipulatives used to model our number system as shown in the figure below. Note that a skinny is made of 10 bits, a flat is made of 100 bits, and a pack is made of 1000 bits.

Base-Ten Shorthand (URG Unit 2)
A graphical representation of the base-ten pieces as shown below.

Nickname	Picture	Shorthand
bit		·
skinny		/
flat		
pack		

Benchmarks (SG Unit 7)
Numbers convenient for comparing and ordering numbers, e.g., $0, \frac{1}{2}, 1$ are convenient benchmarks for comparing and ordering fractions.

Best-Fit Line (URG Unit 3; SG Unit 3)
The line that comes closest to the points on a point graph.

Binning Data (URG Unit 8; SG Unit 8)
Placing data from a data set with a large number of values or large range into intervals in order to more easily see patterns in the data.

Bit (URG Unit 2; SG Unit 2)
A cube that measures 1 cm on each edge.
It is the smallest of the base-ten pieces and is often used to represent 1. (*See also* base-ten pieces.)

C

Cartesian Coordinate System (URG Unit 10; SG Unit 10)
A method of locating points on a flat surface by means of an ordered pair of numbers. This method is named after its originator, René Descartes. (*See also* coordinates.)

Categorical Variable (URG Unit 1; SG Unit 1)
Variables with values that are not numbers. (*See also* variable and value.)

Center of a Circle (URG Unit 14; SG Unit 14)
The point such that every point on a circle is the same distance from it. (*See also* circle.)

Centiwheel (URG Unit 7; SG Unit 7)
A circle divided into 100 equal sections used in exploring fractions, decimals, and percents.

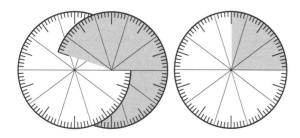

Central Angle (URG Unit 14; SG Unit 14)
An angle whose vertex is at the center of a circle.

Certain Event (URG Unit 7; SG Unit 7)
An event that has a probability of 1 (100%).

Chord (URG Unit 14; SG Unit 14)
A line segment that connects two points on a circle. (*See also* circle.)

Circle (URG Unit 14; SG Unit 14)
A curve that is made up of all the points that are the same distance from one point, the center.

Circumference (URG Unit 14; SG Unit 14)
The distance around a circle.

Common Denominator (URG Unit 5 & Unit 11; SG Unit 5 & Unit 11)
A denominator that is shared by two or more fractions. A common denominator is a common multiple of the denominators of the fractions. 15 is a common denominator of $\frac{2}{3}$ ($= \frac{10}{15}$) and $\frac{4}{5}$ ($= \frac{12}{15}$) since 15 is divisible by both 3 and 5.

Common Fraction (URG Unit 7; SG Unit 7)
Any fraction that is written with a numerator and denominator that are whole numbers. For example, $\frac{3}{4}$ and $\frac{9}{4}$ are both common fractions. (*See also* decimal fraction.)

Commutative Property of Addition (URG Unit 2)
The order of the addends in an addition problem does not matter, e.g., $7 + 3 = 3 + 7$.

Commutative Property of Multiplication (URG Unit 2)
The order of the factors in a multiplication problem does not matter, e.g., $7 \times 3 = 3 \times 7$. (*See also* turn-around facts.)

Compact Method (URG Unit 2)
Another name for what is considered the traditional multiplication algorithm.

$$\begin{array}{r} {\scriptstyle 2\,1} \\ 186 \\ \times\ 3 \\ \hline 558 \end{array}$$

Composite Number (URG Unit 11; SG Unit 11)
A number that has more than two distinct factors. For example, 9 has three factors (1, 3, 9) so it is a composite number.

Concentric Circles (URG Unit 14; SG Unit 14)
Circles that have the same center.

Congruent (URG Unit 6 & Unit 10; SG Unit 6)
Figures that are the same shape and size. Polygons are congruent when corresponding sides have the same length and corresponding angles have the same measure.

Conjecture (URG Unit 11; SG Unit 11)
A statement that has not been proved to be true, nor shown to be false.

Convenient Number (URG Unit 2; SG Unit 2)
A number used in computation that is close enough to give a good estimate, but is also easy to compute with mentally, e.g., 25 and 30 are convenient numbers for 27.

Convex (URG Unit 6)
A shape is convex if for any two points in the shape, the line segment between the points is also inside the shape.

Coordinates (URG Unit 10; SG Unit 10)
An ordered pair of numbers that locates points on a flat surface relative to a pair of coordinate axes. For example, in the ordered pair (4, 5), the first number (coordinate) is the distance from the point to the vertical axis and the second coordinate is the distance from the point to the horizontal axis. (*See also* axes.)

Corresponding Parts (URG Unit 10; SG Unit 10)
Matching parts in two or more figures. In the figure below, Sides AB and A'B' are corresponding parts.

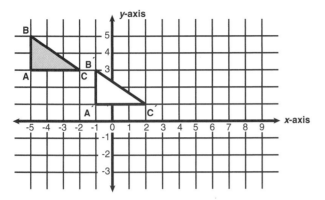

Cryptography (SG Unit 11) The study of secret codes.

Cubic Centimeter (URG Unit 13)
The volume of a cube that is one centimeter long on each edge.

D

Data (SG Unit 1)
Information collected in an experiment or survey.

Decagon (URG Unit 6; SG Unit 6)
A ten-sided, ten-angled polygon.

Decimal (URG Unit 7; SG Unit 7)
1. A number written using the base ten place value system.
2. A number containing a decimal point.

Decimal Fraction (URG Unit 7; SG Unit 7)
A fraction written as a decimal. For example, 0.75 and 0.4 are decimal fractions and $\frac{75}{100}$ and $\frac{4}{10}$ are the equivalent common fractions.

Degree (URG Unit 6; SG Unit 6)
A degree (°) is a unit of measure for angles. There are 360 degrees in a circle.

Denominator (URG Unit 3; SG Unit 3)
The number below the line in a fraction. The denominator indicates the number of equal parts in which the unit whole is divided. For example, the 5 is the denominator in the fraction $\frac{2}{5}$. In this case the unit whole is divided into five equal parts. (*See also* numerator.)

Density (URG Unit 13; SG Unit 13)
The ratio of an object's mass to its volume.

Diagonal (URG Unit 6)
A line segment that connects nonadjacent corners of a polygon.

Diameter (URG Unit 14; SG Unit 14)
1. A line segment that connects two points on a circle and passes through the center.
2. The length of this line segment.

Digit (SG Unit 2)
Any one of the ten symbols 0, 1, 2, 3, 4, 5, 6, 7, 8, 9. The number 37 is made up of the digits 3 and 7.

Dividend (URG Unit 4 & Unit 9; SG Unit 4 & Unit 9)
The number that is divided in a division problem, e.g., 12 is the dividend in 12 ÷ 3 = 4.

Divisor (URG Unit 2, Unit 4, & Unit 9; SG Unit 2, Unit 4, & Unit 9)
In a division problem, the number by which another number is divided. In the problem 12 ÷ 4 = 3, the 4 is the divisor, the 12 is the dividend, and the 3 is the quotient.

Dodecagon (URG Unit 6; SG Unit 6)
A twelve-sided, twelve-angled polygon.

E

Endpoint (URG Unit 6; SG Unit 6)
The point at either end of a line segment or the point at the end of a ray.

Equally Likely (URG Unit 7; SG Unit 7)
When events have the same probability, they are called equally likely.

Equidistant (URG Unit 14)
At the same distance.

Equilateral Triangle (URG Unit 6, Unit 14, & Unit 15)
A triangle that has all three sides equal in length. An equilateral triangle also has three equal angles.

Equivalent Fractions (URG Unit 3; SG Unit 3)
Fractions that have the same value, e.g., $\frac{2}{4} = \frac{1}{2}$.

Estimate (URG Unit 2; SG Unit 2)
1. To find *about* how many (as a verb).
2. A number that is *close to* the desired number (as a noun).

Expanded Form (SG Unit 2)
A way to write numbers that shows the place value of each digit, e.g., 4357 = 4000 + 300 + 50 + 7.

Exponent (URG Unit 2 & Unit 11; SG Unit 2 & Unit 11)
The number of times the base is multiplied by itself. In $3^4 = 3 \times 3 \times 3 \times 3 = 81$, the 3 is the base and the 4 is the exponent. The 3 is multiplied by itself 4 times.

Extrapolation (URG Unit 13; SG Unit 13)
Using patterns in data to make predictions or to estimate values that lie beyond the range of values in the set of data.

F

Fact Families (URG Unit 2; SG Unit 2)
Related math facts, e.g., 3 × 4 = 12, 4 × 3 = 12, 12 ÷ 3 = 4, 12 ÷ 4 = 3.

Factor Tree (URG Unit 11; SG Unit 11)
A diagram that shows the prime factorization of a number.

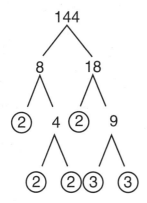

Factors (URG Unit 2 & Unit 11; SG Unit 2 & Unit 11)
1. In a multiplication problem, the numbers that are multiplied together. In the problem $3 \times 4 = 12$, 3 and 4 are the factors.
2. Numbers that divide a number evenly, e.g., 1, 2, 3, 4, 6, and 12 are all the factors of 12.

Fair Game (URG Unit 7; SG Unit 7)
A game in which it is equally likely that any player will win.

Fewest Pieces Rule (URG Unit 2)
Using the least number of base-ten pieces to represent a number. (*See also* base-ten pieces.)

Fixed Variables (URG Unit 4; SG Unit 3 & Unit 4)
Variables in an experiment that are held constant or not changed, in order to find the relationship between the manipulated and responding variables. These variables are often called controlled variables. (*See also* manipulated variable and responding variable.)

Flat (URG Unit 2; SG Unit 2)
A block that measures 1 cm $\times$ 10 cm $\times$ 10 cm. It is one of the base-ten pieces and is often used to represent 100. (*See also* base-ten pieces.)

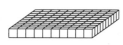

Flip (URG Unit 10; SG Unit 10)
A motion of the plane in which the plane is reflected over a line so that any point and its image are the same distance from the line.

Forgiving Division Method
(URG Unit 4; SG Unit 4)
A paper-and-pencil method for division in which successive partial quotients are chosen and subtracted from the dividend, until the remainder is less than the divisor. The sum of the partial quotients is the quotient. For example, $644 \div 7$ can be solved as shown at the right.

```
        92
   7 )644
      140 | 20
      ---
      504
      350 | 50
      ---
      154
      140 | 20
      ---
       14
       14 |  2
      ---
        0 | 92
```

Formula (SG Unit 11 & Unit 14)
A number sentence that gives a general rule. A formula for finding the area of a rectangle is Area = length $\times$ width, or $A = l \times w$.

Fraction (URG Unit 7; SG Unit 7)
A number that can be written as a/b where a and b are whole numbers and b is not zero.

G

Googol (URG Unit 2)
A number that is written as a 1 with 100 zeroes after it (10^{100}).

Googolplex (URG Unit 2)
A number that is written as a 1 with a googol of zeroes after it.

H

Height of a Triangle (URG Unit 15; SG Unit 15)
A line segment from a vertex of a triangle perpendicular to the opposite side or to the line extending the opposite side; also, the length of this line. The height is also called the altitude.

Hexagon (URG Unit 6; SG Unit 6)
A six-sided polygon.

Hypotenuse (URG Unit 15; SG Unit 15)
The longest side of a right triangle.

I

Image (URG Unit 10; SG Unit 10)
The result of a transformation, in particular a slide (translation) or a flip (reflection), in a coordinate plane. The new figure after the slide or flip is the image of the old figure.

Impossible Event (URG Unit 7; SG Unit 7)
An event that has a probability of 0 or 0%.

Improper Fraction (URG Unit 3; SG Unit 3)
A fraction in which the numerator is greater than or equal to the denominator. An improper fraction is greater than or equal to one.

Infinite (URG Unit 2)
Never ending, immeasurably great, unlimited.

Interpolation (URG Unit 13; SG Unit 13)
Making predictions or estimating values that lie between data points in a set of data.

Intersect (URG Unit 14)
To meet or cross.

Isosceles Triangle (URG Unit 6 & Unit 15)
A triangle that has at least two sides of equal length.

J

K

L

Lattice Multiplication
(URG Unit 9; SG Unit 9)
A method for multiplying that
uses a lattice to arrange the
partial products so the digits are
correctly placed in the correct
place value columns. A lattice
for 43 × 96 = 4128 is shown at
the right.

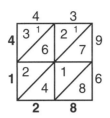

Legs of a Right Triangle (URG Unit 15; SG Unit 15)
The two sides of a right triangle that form the right angle.

Length of a Rectangle (URG Unit 4 & Unit 15;
SG Unit 4 & Unit 15)
The distance along one side of a rectangle.

Line
A set of points that form a straight path extending infi-
nitely in two directions.

Line of Reflection (URG Unit 10)
A line that acts as a mirror so that after a shape is flipped
over the line, corresponding points are at the same distance (equidistant) from the line.

Line Segment (URG Unit 14)
A part of a line between and including two points, called
the endpoints.

Liter (URG Unit 13)
Metric unit used to measure volume. A liter is a little
more than a quart.

Lowest Terms (SG Unit 11)
A fraction is in lowest terms if the numerator and
denominator have no common factor greater than 1.

M

Manipulated Variable (URG Unit 4; SG Unit 4)
In an experiment, the variable with values known at the
beginning of the experiment. The experimenter often
chooses these values before data is collected. The manipulated variable is often called the independent variable.

Mass (URG Unit 13)
The amount of matter in an object.

Mean (URG Unit 1 & Unit 4; SG Unit 1 & Unit 4)
An average of a set of numbers that is found by adding
the values of the data and dividing by the number of
values.

Measurement Division (URG Unit 4)
Division as equal grouping. The total number of objects
and the number of objects in each group are known. The
number of groups is the unknown. For example, tulip
bulbs come in packages of 8. If 216 bulbs are sold, how
many packages are sold?

Median (URG Unit 1; SG Unit 1)
For a set with an odd number of data arranged in order,
it is the middle number. For an even number of data
arranged in order, it is the mean of the two middle
numbers.

Meniscus (URG Unit 13)
The curved surface formed when a liquid creeps up the
side of a container (for example, a graduated cylinder).

Milliliter (ml) (URG Unit 13)
A measure of capacity in the metric system that is the
volume of a cube that is one centimeter long on each
side.

Mixed Number (URG Unit 3; SG Unit 3)
A number that is written as a whole number followed by
a fraction. It is equal to the sum of the whole number and
the fraction.

Mode (URG Unit 1; SG Unit 1)
The most common value in a data set.

Mr. Origin (URG Unit 10; SG Unit 10)
A plastic figure used to represent the origin of a coordinate system and to indicate the directions of the x- and
y- axes. (and possibly the z-axis).

N

N-gon (URG Unit 6; SG Unit 6)
A polygon with N sides.

Negative Number (URG Unit 10; SG Unit 10)
A number less than zero; a number to the left of zero on a
horizontal number line.

Nonagon (URG Unit 6; SG Unit 6)
A nine-sided polygon.

Numerator (URG Unit 3; SG Unit 3)
The number written above the line in a fraction. For
example, the 2 is the numerator in the fraction $\frac{2}{5}$. In this
case, we are interested in two of the five parts. (*See also*
denominator.)

Numerical Expression (URG Unit 4; SG Unit 4)
A combination of numbers and operations, e.g.,
$5 + 8 \div 4$.

Numerical Variable (URG Unit 1; SG Unit 1)
Variables with values that are numbers. (*See also* variable
and value.)

O

Obtuse Angle (URG Unit 6; SG Unit 6)
An angle that measures more than 90°.

Obtuse Triangle (URG Unit 6 & Unit 15; SG Unit 6 & Unit 15)
A triangle that has an obtuse angle.

Octagon (URG Unit 6; SG Unit 6)
An eight-sided polygon.

Ordered Pair (URG Unit 10; SG Unit 10)
A pair of numbers that gives the coordinates of a point on a grid in relation to the origin. The horizontal coordinate is given first; the vertical coordinate is given second. For example, the ordered pair (5, 3) gives the coordinates of the point that is 5 units to the right of the origin and 3 units up.

Origin (URG Unit 10; SG Unit 10)
The point at which the *x*- and *y*-axes intersect on a coordinate plane. The origin is described by the ordered pair (0, 0) and serves as a reference point so that all the points on the plane can be located by ordered pairs.

P

Pack (URG Unit 2; SG Unit 2)
A cube that measures 10 cm on each edge. It is one of the base-ten pieces and is often used to represent 1000. (*See also* base-ten pieces.)

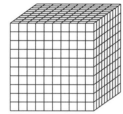

Parallel Lines
  (URG Unit 6 & Unit 10)
Lines that are in the same direction. In the plane, parallel lines are lines that do not intersect.

Parallelogram (URG Unit 6)
A quadrilateral with two pairs of parallel sides.

Partial Product (URG Unit 2)
One portion of the multiplication process in the all-partials multiplication method, e.g., in the problem 3 × 186 there are three partial products: 3 × 6 = 18, 3 × 80 = 240, and 3 × 100 = 300. (*See also* all-partials multiplication method.)

Partitive Division (URG Unit 4)
Division as equal sharing. The total number of objects and the number of groups are known. The number of objects in each group is the unknown. For example, Frank has 144 marbles that he divides equally into 6 groups. How many marbles are in each group?

Pentagon (URG Unit 6; SG Unit 6)
A five-sided polygon.

Percent (URG Unit 7; SG Unit 7)
Per hundred or out of 100. A special ratio that compares a number to 100. For example, 20% (twenty percent) of the jelly beans are yellow means that out of every 100 jelly beans, 20 are yellow.

Perimeter (URG Unit 15; SG Unit 15)
The distance around a two-dimensional shape.

Period (SG Unit 2)
A group of three places in a large number, starting on the right, often separated by commas as shown at the right.

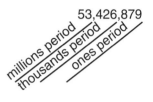

Perpendicular Lines (URG Unit 14 & Unit 15; SG Unit 14)
Lines that meet at right angles.

Pi (π) (URG Unit 14; SG Unit 14)
The ratio of the circumference to diameter of a circle. π = 3.14159265358979. . . . It is a nonterminating, nonrepeating decimal.

Place (SG Unit 2)
The position of a digit in a number.

Place Value (URG Unit 2; SG Unit 2)
The value of a digit in a number. For example, the 5 is in the hundreds place in 4573, so it stands for 500.

Polygon (URG Unit 6; SG Unit 6)
A two-dimensional connected figure made of line segments in which each endpoint of every side meets with an endpoint of exactly one other side.

Population (URG Unit 1 Unit 1)
A collection of persons or things whose properties will be analyzed in a survey or experiment.

Portfolio (URG Unit 2; SG Unit 2)
A collection of student work that show how a student's skills, attitudes, and knowledge change over time.

Positive Number (URG Unit 10; SG Unit 10)
A number greater than zero; a number to the right of zero on a horizontal number line.

Power (URG Unit 2; SG Unit 2)
An exponent. Read 10^4 as, "ten to the fourth power" or "ten to the fourth." We say 10,000 or 10^4 is the fourth power of ten.

Prime Factorization (URG Unit 11; SG Unit 11)
Writing a number as a product of primes. The prime factorization of 100 is 2 × 2 × 5 × 5.

Prime Number (URG Unit 11; SG Unit 11)
A number that has exactly two factors: itself and 1. For example, 7 has exactly two distinct factors, 1 and 7.

Probability (URG Unit 7; SG Unit 1 & Unit 7)
A number from 0 to 1 (0% to 100%) that describes how likely an event is to happen. The closer that the probability of an event is to one, the more likely the event will happen.

Product (URG Unit 2; SG Unit 2)
The answer to a multiplication problem. In the problem $3 \times 4 = 12$, 12 is the product.

Proper Fraction (URG Unit 3; SG Unit 3)
A fraction in which the numerator is less than the denominator. Proper fractions are less than one.

Proportion (URG Unit 3 & Unit 13; SG Unit 13)
A statement that two ratios are equal.

Protractor (URG Unit 6; SG Unit 6)
A tool for measuring angles.

Q

Quadrants (URG Unit 10; SG Unit 10)
The four sections of a coordinate grid that are separated by the axes.

Quadrilateral (URG Unit 6; SG Unit 6)
A polygon with four sides. (*See also* polygon.)

Quotient (URG Unit 4 & Unit 9; SG Unit 2, Unit 4, & Unit 9)
The answer to a division problem. In the problem $12 \div 3 = 4$, the 4 is the quotient.

R

Radius (URG Unit 14; SG Unit 14)
1. A line segment connecting the center of a circle to any point on the circle.
2. The length of this line segment.

Ratio (URG Unit 3 & Unit 12; SG Unit 3 & Unit 13)
A way to compare two numbers or quantities using division. It is often written as a fraction.

Ray (URG Unit 6; SG Unit 6)
A part of a line with one endpoint that extends indefinitely in one direction.

Rectangle (URG Unit 6; SG Unit 6)
A quadrilateral with four right angles.

Reflection (URG Unit 10)
(*See* flip.)

Regular Polygon (URG Unit 6; SG Unit 6; DAB Unit 6)
A polygon with all sides of equal length and all angles equal.

Remainder (URG Unit 4 & Unit 9; SG Unit 4 & Unit 9)
Something that remains or is left after a division problem. The portion of the dividend that is not evenly divisible by the divisor, e.g., $16 \div 5 = 3$ with 1 as a remainder.

Repeating Decimals (SG Unit 9)
A decimal fraction with one or more digits repeating without end.

Responding Variable (URG Unit 4; SG Unit 4)
The variable whose values result from the experiment. Experimenters find the values of the responding variable by doing the experiment. The responding variable is often called the dependent variable.

Rhombus (URG Unit 6; SG Unit 6)
A quadrilateral with four equal sides.

Right Angle (URG Unit 6; SG Unit 6)
An angle that measures 90°.

Right Triangle (URG Unit 6 & Unit 15; SG Unit 6 & Unit 15)
A triangle that contains a right angle.

Rubric (URG Unit 1)
A scoring guide that can be used to guide or assess student work.

S

Sample (URG Unit 1)
A part or subset of a population.

Scalene Triangle (URG Unit 15)
A triangle that has no sides that are equal in length.

Scientific Notation (URG Unit 2; SG Unit 2)
A way of writing numbers, particularly very large or very small numbers. A number in scientific notation has two factors. The first factor is a number greater than or equal to one and less than ten. The second factor is a power of 10 written with an exponent. For example, 93,000,000 written in scientific notation is 9.3×10^7.

Septagon (URG Unit 6; SG Unit 6)
A seven-sided polygon.

Side-Angle-Side (URG Unit 6 & Unit 14)
A geometric property stating that two triangles having two corresponding sides with the included angle equal are congruent.

Side-Side-Side (URG Unit 6)
A geometric property stating that two triangles having corresponding sides equal are congruent.

Sides of an Angle (URG Unit 6; SG Unit 6)
The sides of an angle are two rays with the same endpoint. (*See also* endpoint and ray.)

Sieve of Eratosthenes (SG Unit 11)
A method for separating prime numbers from nonprime numbers developed by Eratosthenes, an Egyptian librarian, in about 240 BCE.

Similar (URG Unit 6; SG Unit 6)
Similar shapes have the same shape but not necessarily the same size.

Skinny (URG Unit 2; SG Unit 2)
A block that measures 1 cm × 1 cm × 10 cm.
It is one of the base-ten pieces
and is often used to represent 10.
(*See also* base-ten pieces.)

Slide (URG Unit 10; SG Unit 10)
Moving a geometric figure in the plane by moving every point of the figure the same distance in the same direction. Also called translation.

Speed (URG Unit 3 & Unit 5; SG Unit 3 & Unit 5)
The ratio of distance moved to time taken, e.g.,
3 miles/1 hour or 3 mph is a speed.

Square (URG Unit 6 & Unit 14; SG Unit 6)
A quadrilateral with four equal sides and four right angles.

Square Centimeter (URG Unit 4; SG Unit 4)
The area of a square that is 1 cm long on each side.

Square Number (URG Unit 11)
A number that is the product of a whole number multiplied by itself. For example, 25 is a square number since $5 \times 5 = 25$. A square number can be represented by a square array with the same number of rows as columns. A square array for 25 has 5 rows of 5 objects in each row or 25 total objects.

Standard Form (SG Unit 2)
The traditional way to write a number, e.g., standard form for three hundred fifty-seven is 357. (*See also* expanded form and word form.)

Standard Units (URG Unit 4)
Internationally or nationally agreed-upon units used in measuring variables, e.g., centimeters and inches are standard units used to measure length and square centimeters and square inches are used to measure area.

Straight Angle (URG Unit 6; SG Unit 6)
An angle that measures 180°.

T

Ten Percent (URG Unit 4; SG Unit 4)
10 out of every hundred or $\frac{1}{10}$.

Tessellation (URG Unit 6 & Unit 10; SG Unit 6)
A pattern made up of one or more repeated shapes that completely covers a surface without any gaps or overlaps.

Translation
(*See* slide.)

Trapezoid (URG Unit 6)
A quadrilateral with exactly one pair of parallel sides.

Triangle (URG Unit 6; SG Unit 6)
A polygon with three sides.

Triangulating (URG Unit 6; SG Unit 6)
Partitioning a polygon into two or more nonoverlapping triangles by drawing diagonals that do not intersect.

Turn-Around Facts (URG Unit 2)
Multiplication facts that have the same factors but in a different order, e.g., $3 \times 4 = 12$ and $4 \times 3 = 12$. (*See also* commutative property of multiplication.)

Twin Primes (URG Unit 11; SG Unit 11)
A pair of prime numbers whose difference is 2. For example, 3 and 5 are twin primes.

U

Unit Ratio (URG Unit 13; SG Unit 13)
A ratio with a denominator of one.

V

Value (URG Unit 1; SG Unit 1)
The possible outcomes of a variable. For example, red, green, and blue are possible values for the variable *color*. Two meters and 1.65 meters are possible values for the variable *length*.

Variable (URG Unit 1; SG Unit 1)
1. An attribute or quantity that changes or varies. (*See also* categorical variable and numerical variable.)
2. A symbol that can stand for a variable.

Variables in Proportion (URG Unit 13; SG Unit 13)
When the ratio of two variables in an experiment is always the same, the variables are in proportion.

Velocity (URG Unit 5; SG Unit 5)
Speed in a given direction. Speed is the ratio of the distance traveled to time taken.

Vertex (URG Unit 6; SG Unit 6)
A common point of two rays or line segments that form an angle.

Volume (URG Unit 13)
The measure of the amount of space occupied by an object.

W

Whole Number
Any of the numbers 0, 1, 2, 3, 4, 5, 6 and so on.

Width of a Rectangle (URG Unit 4 & Unit 15; SG Unit 4 & Unit 15)
The distance along one side of a rectangle is the length and the distance along an adjacent side is the width.

Word Form (SG Unit 2)
A number expressed in words, e.g., the word form for 123 is "one hundred twenty-three." (*See also* expanded form and standard form.)

X

Y

Z